MW01627344

ANIMALS AND THE CHURCH

GERALD JONES

2003

EBORN BOOKS

SALT LAKE CITY, UTAH

ANIMALS AND THE CHURCH

Limited Edition of 500 Copies

Library of Congress Catalog No.2003093286
ISBN: 1-890718-26-2

Distributed by Eborn Books, 433 E. Broadway,
Salt Lake City, Utah, 84111.
ebornbk@doitnow.com
www.ebornbooks.com

Printed in the United States of America

Acknowledgments

Thirty years ago I received encouragement from Roy Doxey and Milton V. Backman Jr. Professor Backman chaired my dissertation committee on which this book is based.

Scott Smith believed in the importance of the work and published an earlier version in 1980 which soon sold out.

Greg Anderson prodigiously put the major portion on the computer. Bret Eborn saw the value of the work and prepared it for publication.

Finally, my wife Joyce and my five living children, Eric, JanEtta, Nadine, Sylvia, and Gerald L. Have encouraged me to submit it for publication. So family and friends, here it is! Thanks to all!

— Gerald E. Jones

Contents

Preface

I cannot single out just one day as the one that changed my life. There have been many. It is interesting that many of them are centered on my involvement with animals and a concern for their well-being.

Born to college-educated parents living on a farm in central South Dakota during the depression years of the 1930s would not have seemed a promising beginning to one becoming an animals' advocate. Nonetheless the lifestyle made its impact in various ways. Food was scarce and my father hunted rabbits and pheasants frequently to feed his wife and three children. Cattle, hogs, and chickens were raised for food or sale to buy other necessities of life. Sometimes he would trap predators for their skins to sell. Life was not easy on a farm a dozen miles or so from the nearest store.

As I grew up I became more like my father—a farm boy who loved to read. As the oldest child I also helped to provide for the family. I soon learned to hunt with a rifle given to me by my grandfather, who also farmed nearby. By the time I was in high school I had a reputation for being a sharpshooter, able to shoot pheasants on the wing with my .22 caliber rifle. Gophers, prairie dogs, and any creature that seemed to compete with our livelihood were "fair game."

While in elementary school, a one-room, one-teacher-for-all-eight-grades school, I became involved in the 4-H program. Projects included raising a small plot of wheat, some registered hogs, and calves. One year the county fathers sponsored a calf-roping contest among a bunch of the 4-H boys. Those fortunate enough to rope a calf at the county fair were able to keep it and turn back its first calf to the fair committee to keep the program supplied for future contests. That calf I caught became a real pet and as a cow was very devoted to me. It would come when called and would follow me around if allowed (inside the house was off limits, though it tried to come in a few times). The same was true of my pigs. I seemed to enjoy them, and they responded with affection and attention.

During these elementary school years I would walk to school on our country road about two-thirds of a mile. A pet cat, Niger, would often come part way to meet me coming home. She would jump upon my shoulder and ride home curled around my neck, purring all the way. She would have me help her hunt mice. On my shoulder she would wait for me to turn over boards on the ground and then jump on a mouse that tried to scurry away. Sometimes my grandmother would have me shoot sparrows from the eaves, and the cat would sit on my shoulder until I shot; it would then jump down to eat the fallen sparrow.

These early experiences caused me to ponder my relationships to animal life. The trust and feelings I received from many of our animals made it difficult for me to kill them for food for the family. I also began to realize it was definitely not sport nor fun to kill with a rifle. The odds were not fair by any stretch of the imagination. I stopped hunting for sport.

It was about this time, during my beginning teenage years, that I became acquainted with The Church of Jesus Christ of Latter-day Saints. I was surprised to find that Joseph Smith taught that humans should be kind to the animal world. One famous incident was when a group of men known as Zion's Camp were going from Ohio to Missouri to help alleviate the persecution of the Church members. En route they found some rattlesnakes and were about to kill them when Joseph stopped them with the injunction not to kill any living creature unless necessary to protect human life. The snakes could be avoided and removed without harming them and so that is what was done. He further implied that the peaceful millennial reign of Christ could not take place until people learned to be kind to all living creatures first. There was a direct implication that Isaiah's prophecy in Isaiah 11:6-9 and 65:25 was partly humanity's responsibility to set the moral climate for this peace between animals and humans and each other. One of the revelations in the Doctrine and Covenants, section 77, stated that animals have spirits and will be resurrected. This, of course, is a radical departure from traditional Christian church views. It was another reason for me to rethink my views of life. I decided not to hunt anymore and gradually withdrew from any farm activity that would cause harm to any living creature. This was not easy to do. Peer pressure, family pressure, teasing , and some farm activity required patience and tact.

A class in ethics at the university allowed me to read more on social concerns. A two-year mission for the Church was followed by a return to school, where I began to write term papers on the subject of animals and our treatment of them. History, theology, philosophy, and sociology all allowed a varied perspective and broadened my understanding of the humane movement. Graduate school with a major in the history and philosophy of religion and a minor in philosophy again allowed me to read extensively in world religions and Christianity and secular philosophers, where I was able to glean more information on a topic that many thought was weird, extreme, impractical, and of no interest to anyone else they knew. My thesis compared Alan Watts and Paul Tillich, both of whom I met and who later signed my copy. Tillich was a guest lecturer for six weeks at the University of Iowa school of religion, which I attended. His "ground of being" and Watts's Buddhist and Taoist views resonated with my interest. Lack of money and support for my studies left me with no choice but to return to BYU to finish my Ph.D. At the Y I found the dean of the school of religion, Roy Doxey, had become aware of the validity of my research and agreed that I could do my dissertation on the subject. There was opposition from some in the graduate school, but with his support I prevailed.

The dissertation began with some background of concern for animals in philosophy and religion historically, both eastern and western. Ahimsa and Schweitzer's "reverence for life" were highlights, but there is a plethora of material from the ancient to modern thinkers in both secular and religious fields. I then decided to go into depth with five American churches: Bible Christian, Seventh-Day Adventist, Christian Science, Shakers, and The Church of Jesus Christ of Latter-day Saints. The first two were vegetarian oriented, though the Bible Christians did apply the fifth commandment, "thou shalt not kill," to all forms of life. The Christian Scientists had the least commentary on the subject, while the Latter-day Saints had the most by far, more than all the others combined. From Joseph Smith and Brigham Young to David O. McKay and Spencer W. Kimball there has been a strong emphasis on being kind to animals and birds and not hunting for sport, which was considered a sin. The Church magazine, the *Ensign*, published my article on the gospel and animals in 1972 and in 1977 printed some answers to questions on the subject. I was also invited to deliver Know Your Religion lectures on the topic in Southern California. When attempting to publish a book on the subject, I was rejected and the project was deemed not economically feasible. About this time, I received a call from Scott Smith, who asked if he could publish the LDS-related chapters of the dissertation. Even though I have still never met Scott personally, I appreciated his confidence. He published two thousand copies which sold out in about a year. Due to problems with his distributor, lack of funds, and the feeling the market was saturated it was not republished. But many requests came and still do after eighteen years. It is time to publish it again with revisions and additions.

Chapter 1

Introduction

Mankind's recorded history manifests many ways and degrees of concern for animals. The flesh of animals was considered important as food in supporting human life. Domestication served to keep a supply of food at hand. Animals were trained to provide services for man such as protection, travel, and various tasks for which animal labor could be utilized. Primitive religions often regarded animals as sacred totems or representative of deity. Animals have also been considered as the embodiment of evil forces. Mythology frequently has identified animals with the origins of mankind, discussing important influences in the various relationships of animals to man.[1]

Mankind's desire to show kindness to the animal kingdom is referred to with terms such as *humanitarianism*, *reverence for life*, and *zoophily*. These terms are used synonymously in this study.[2] The primary concern of this study is man's kindness to animals, particularly as demonstrated by the teachings and programs of five churches that have a basically American development.

---

1 Evelyn Martinengo Cesaresco, *The Place of Animals in Human Thought* (New York: Scribner's and Sons, 1909). Also see Richard Lewinsohn, *Animals, Men and Myths* (New York: Harper & Bros.,1954).

2 The primary connotation of *zoophilist* in *Webster's Third New International Dictionary*, unabridged (Springfield: G. & C. Merriam Co., 1966), is preferred to the other connotations found under related headings. This is supported by Funk and Wagnall's *New Standard Dictionary* (New York: Funk and Wagnall, 1960), and the *Oxford English Dictionary*, vol. XII (Oxford: University Press, 1961), both of which ignore the other connotations of Webster.

Zoophily in the Judeo-Christian culture has usually manifested itself in the form of organizations that are not basically oriented to organized religion or churches. Basically four concepts have contributed to the Western reverence for the life of animals among the secular organizations sponsoring zoophilic ideals. Though these four concepts are religious in nature, they are not found in the formal creeds of the larger Christian denominations of European origin. The major rationale prompting kindness to animals is the evolutionary concept of man and animals belonging to one large family.[3]

A second principle is the premise that kindness practiced to animals will result in greater kindness to mankind.[4] Vegetarianism has been a third motivating factor to the practice of zoophily. Even though vegetarianism may be practiced strictly for the benefit of human health, it has resulted in a sparing of animal life.[5] Finally, there is the rarer concept that animals will have a place in a life hereafter and man will be held accountable by God for his treatment of these eternal creatures.[6]

---

3 Henry Stephens Salt, *The Creed of Kinship* (New York: E. P. Dutton & Co., 1935), 1-2, 55-57.

4 Ibid., 47-53. See Philip P. Hallie, *The Paradox of Cruelty* (Middletown, Conn.: Wesleyan University Press, 1969), and Thomas Aquinas, *Summa Theologica* (Chicago: Encyclopedia Britannica Great Books, 1952), I, 502-510, and Martin Luther, *Luther's Works* (St. Louis: Concordia Publishing House, 1960), IX, 220.

5 Martin E. Coville, *An Appeal Against Slaughter* (Syracuse: C.W. Bardeen Publishers, 1914). Also Geoffrey L. Rudd, *Why Kill for Food*?(Wilmslow, Cheshire: The Vegetarian Society, 1956); Howard Williams, *The Ethics of Diet* (London: F. Pitman, 1883); and F.J. Simoons, *Eat Not This Flesh: Food Avoidances in the Old World* (Madison: University of Wisconsin Press, 1961); Joseph Ritson, *An Essay on Abstinence from Animal Food as a Moral Duty* (London: R. Phillips, 1802).

6 Noah J. Cohen, *Tsa'ar Ba'ale Hayim—The Prevention of Cruelty to Animals: Its Basis, Development and Legislation in Hebrew Literature*

The kinship of animals to mankind as being fellow creatures in the same general family has long been a reason for showing kindness to animals. Among the Asian religions of Hinduism, Buddhism, and Jainism are found the beliefs of reincarnation or the transmigration of souls. The belief that a soul may be born as an animal and then later return as a human, or that a human may later be born as an animal encourages kindness towards these fellow beings.[7] The doctrine of "ahimsa" in Jainism is the most developed practice of kindness to all living things. The Jains are noted for their animal hospitals, their very meticulous avoidance of injury to animals or insects and strict vegetarian diets.[8]

The Western world had an early spokesman for the transmigration theory and the resultant need for kindness to animal life. Pythagoras, 570-470 B.C., was a Greek philosopher whose ideas influenced Plato and the fields of mathematics and mysticism. His doctrine of metem-psychosis was a basis for treating animals kindly. Pythagoras held that animals had souls of past or future humans, therefore eating animal flesh was "unnatural and unlawful," since animals were

---

(Washington, D.C.: The Catholic University of America Press, 1959). Also see E.D. Buckner, *The Immortality of Animals and the Relation of Man as Guardian* (Philadelphia: George W. Jacobs & Co., 1903); Agnes Carr, *The Animals and Birds Redeemed from Death: Their Eternal Glory* (San Francisco: n.n., 1953); Dix Harwood, *Love for Animals* (New York: n.n., 1928), 145-60, and later references pertaining to the Shakers and Latter-day Saints.

7 Sarvepalli Radhakrishnan, *Indian Philosophy* (New York: MacMillan & Co., 1929), I, 220, 293-94, 320-25. See also John Noss, *Man's Religions* (New York: MacMillan & Co., 1956), 144-45, 164-65, 225; and Sarvepalli Radhakrishnan and Charles A.Moore, *A Source Book in Indian Philosophy* (Princeton: Princeton University Press, 1957), 77, 108, 165, 198.

8 Radhakrishnan and Moore, 251, 259; Noss, 144-45, 150-52.

"fraternal" beings.[9]

The belief that animals were closely related to man and therefore treated as brothers was argued by Celsus, the second-century Greek critic of Christianity. With sharp insight, Celsus pointed out that animals, rather than man, may be the center of the universe. Criticizing Christian anthropocentrism, Celsus contended that men and animals were equally important in the universal scheme of things. Other fragments of Celsus's writings contain examples of characteristics and abilities which provoke admiration for animals. He concluded his argument for the concern of animal life with the idea that "everything was created not in the interest of something else, but to contribute to the harmony of the whole in order that the world might be absolutely perfect."[10]

The third-century Neoplatonist, Plotinus, also gave credence to the kinship of animals to man. In speaking of the animating force within animals, Plotinus speculated on two possibilities: "If there be no human soul in them, the animate is constituted for them by a radiation from the All-Soul."[11] Either alternative gave strong support for kindness to animals. Porphyry, the ardent disciple of Plotinus, felt that "justice consists in not injuring anything" which included all animate beings. Further, he contended, the power of reason was not unique with man but was shared by animals and indeed, some animals approached perfection in rational activity.[12] Porphyry is credited with writing one of the earliest

---

9 Ovid, *Metempsychosis* (Cambridge: Harvard University Press, 1916), 369-93, 399. See also Herbert Strainge Long, *A Study of the Doctrine of Metempsychosis in Greece from Pythagoras to Plato* (Princeton: Princeton University Press, 1948).

10 Origen, *"Against Celsus," Ante-Nicene Fathers* (Grand Rapids: Wm. B. Eerdmans, 1953), IV, 541. Hereafter *ANF*.

11 Plotinus, *Enneads* (Boston: Charles T. Ranford, 1916), 39.

12 Porphyry, *On Abstinence from Animal Food* (New York: Barnes & Noble, 1965), 109-22.

essays on "abstinence from animal food," which was a logical conclusion to his concept of animals as part of the creation of God and a near equal to man.[13]

The principle of man's kindness to animals resulting in man's kindness to man was taught by early humanitarians. Many taught that cruelty to animals led to cruelty to humanity. Pythagoras held that some "ill exemplar" filled mankind's "greedy paunch" with animals' flesh and thus "opened the road for crime." He further held that those who are accustomed to abominate the slaughter of animals, thinking it iniquitous and unnatural, will think it even more unlawful to kill a man or to engage in war.[14] And Seneca, the rejected Roman counselor to Nero, taught that "cruelty is formed whenever butchery is practiced to the gratification of the appetite."[15]

Porphyry also felt cruelty toward mankind was learned from the way man treated animals. He held it was those who killed animals for meat who later became robbers, tyrants, and murderers.[16]

Giovanni Francesco Bernardone, born in Italy in 1182, later became renowned as the benefactor of animals, popularly known as Saint Francis of Assisi. There are many stories about St. Francis which, probably, must be discredited for lack of historical evidence. However, the stories still indicate the type of man he was and his attitude toward animals. One of the more famous stories shows him befriending a bad wolf and eventually making a household companion of it. Another story portrays him buying some caged doves from their peddler only to set them free. He is also said to have preached to a flock of birds, lifted worms from his path to avoid stepping on them, and taken honey and wine to the bees

---

13 Ibid., 123-44; Long, 22-23.

14 Ovid, 373.

15 Lucius Seneca, *The Epistles* (Cambridge: Harvard University Press, 1943), III, 241.

16 Porphyry, op. cit.

in the winter season to keep them from expiring.[17] Although Roman Catholic doctrine did not teach a kinship concept of animals, Francis was a great exponent and practitioner of kindness to all, including animals.

Thomas Aquinas, the great philosophical systematizer of thirteenth-century Catholic theology, advocated kindness with a caution. According to Thomas, the important thing was not the rights or feelings of the animals but rather the attitude of man that needed training. He thus recommended moderated kindness to animals as a step to increased kindness to humans, but did not advocate zoophily as a practice "deserved" by animals in any way.[18]

Another theologian, the reformer Martin Luther, in his commentary on Deuteronomy 26:6 stated that "by the kind treatment of animals they [Christians] are to learn gentleness and kindness."[19] Luther, however, said very little on the subject of animals in his many works.[20]

The early utopian, Thomas More, published his plan for a perfect society in 1516. Finding fault with the so-called pleasures of hunters, he said hunting was "a thing unworthy to be used of free men" and consequently should be abandoned. Butchers were considered the lower rung in their utopian society because of their constant association with death and cruelty to animals. Others were to avoid cruelty to animals because they "had no affinity with true and right feeling," and, he added, long exposure would result in cruelty to man.[21]

An early French exponent of zoophily was Michel de Montaigne.

---

17 St. Francis of Assisi, *The Little Flowers of St. Francis* (New York: E. P. Dutton & Co., 1951), 36-39, 50-54. See also Martinengo Cesaresco, 257-60.

18 Aquinas, *Summa Theologica*, 383-84, 510.

19 Martin Luther, *Luther's Works* (St. Louis: Concordia Publishing House, 1960), IX, 220.

20 Harwood, refers to a story of Luther reassuring a sorrowing girl that her pet dog would be resurrected and live in heaven, 145-46.

21 Thomas More, *Utopia* (New York: P.E. Collier & Son, 1910), 200-201.

This popular essayist of the sixteenth century firmly believed that men who enjoyed "spectacles of the slaughter of animals" soon "proceeded to those of the slaughter of men." Influenced by Pythagoras, Montaigne did not accept the Pythagorean reincarnation concepts but he did advocate humane treatment of animals and cited humorous historical precedents for such concern.[22]

Two centuries later, an English jurist, logician, and philosopher also advocated zoophily for the sake of the moral lessons to be learned and practiced. Jeremy Bentham wrote concerning the barbarous spectacles in Rome which "without doubt contributed to give the Romans that ferocity which they displayed in their civil wars." For this reason, Bentham contended, it is proper "to forbid every kind of cruelty exercised towards animals." Coming under condemnation by Bentham were the popular sports of the day in England such as "cockfights, bull-baiting, hunting hares and foxes, fishing and other amusements" that tended to dull the sensibilities to pain in mankind.[23] Zoophilists have often quoted a phrase of Bentham given in a footnote wherein he asked concerning cruelty to animals: "The question is not, can they reason? nor, can they talk? but, can they suffer?"[24]

In 1751 the English engraver, William Hogarth, presented a graphic study of human cruelty to animals and mankind in his "Four Stages of Cruelty." The first of four engravings depicted the pleasure men received from torturing animals. In the remaining scenes Hogarth portrayed what he felt was the result of animal cruelty—cruelty to other human beings.[25]

---

22 Michel Montaigne, *Essays* (Chicago: Encyclopedia Britannica Great Books, 1952), XXV, 206-8.

23 Jeremy Bentham, *The Works of Jeremy Bentham* (New York: Russell and Russell, Inc., 1962), I, 562.

24 Ibid., 143; emphasis in original.

25 Philip P. Hallie, *The Paradox of Cruelty* (Middletown, Connecticut: Wesleyan University Press, 1969), 20-33.

Hogarth's engravings have been given credit for motivating later legislation in England protecting animals.[26]

England was the first country to provide parliamentary laws protecting animals from cruelty. Richard Martin introduced the bill commonly called "Humanity Martin's Cattle Bill," which was incorporated into English law in 1882. Many amendments and supplementary laws have been added since to English law extending animals' rights for kinder treatment.[27] England has led the world in general interest and activity on the subject of zoophily and was the home of worldwide organizations such as the Society for the Prevention of Cruelty to Animals, Bands of Mercy, and Vegetarian societies.[28] The related interest in America was definitely influenced by the activity in England and is discussed later in this work.[29]

Since the days of the early Greeks, the two major reasons given for zoophily—kinship to animals and the practice of kindness—have had proponents of both secular and religious persuasions. Vegetarianism has had many advocates since the days of the Greek Pythagoras referred to earlier. The earliest extant essay advocating a flesh-free diet was written by Plutarch about the end of the first century A.D. Plutarch's reasons for abstaining from meat are for better health, kindness engendered, and

---

26 E. S. Turner, *All Heaven in a Rage* (New York: St. Martin's Press, 1965), 51-56, 116-17.

27 Emily Stewart Leavitt, *Animals and Their Legal Rights* (New York: Animal Welfare Institute, 1968), 11; Roswell Cheney McCrea, *The Humane Movement* (New York: Columbia University Press, 1910), 30-32; Francis H. Rowley, *The Humane Idea* (Boston: American Humane Society, 1912), 33-35. The English law, known also as "Martin's Act," allowed magistrates to fine an offender up to five pounds or three months' imprisonment for cruel treatment to cattle, horses, and sheep.

28 Rowley, 35-65.

29 Harwood gives an excellent summary of how zoophily developed in Great Britain and indicates the ways by which America was influenced.

man's natural physical and mental makeup that are adapted to a vegetarian diet.[30]

One of the early Christian proponents of the fleshless diet was Jerome, translator of the Greek Bible into the Latin vulgate. Near the end of the fourth century, Jerome wrote against the heretic Jovinianus, and in doing so was careful to state that he, Jerome, was not a follower of Empedocles and Pythagoras, "who do not eat any living creature" because of their belief in the transmigration of souls. Nevertheless, Jerome closes his comments on eating flesh with the words: "And so I too say to you: If you wish to be perfect, it is good not to drink wine, and eat flesh." He also advised that meat was permissible for those who need strength such as athletes, rhetoricians, soldiers, and the like, but followers of wisdom do not need it.[31]

A noted seventeenth-century advocate of vegetarianism was John Evelyn, an English writer. *Acetaria* was one of his now rare works and dealt with his belief in salads for a diet.[32] Another Englishman, Thomas Tryon, followed shortly with a number of publications concerning vegetarianism including three volumes on *The Way to Health, Long Life, Etc.*, which was published between 1683 and 1697. Other early English advocates of the meatless meal were John Ray, Bernard de Mandeville, John Gay, George Cheyne, and Alexander Pope.[33] John Wesley, who helped to found the Methodist Church, practiced vegetarianism for a brief period of his life.[34]

---

30 Plutarch, *Lives and Writings* (New York: Colonial Co., 1905), X, 3-16.

31 Jerome, "Against Jovinianus," *Nicene and Post-Nicene Fathers* (New York: Christian Literature Co., 1895), VI, 391-94.

32 Williams, 1108-10.

33 Ibid., 113-32.

34 John Wesley, *The Works of John Wesley* (London: Wesleyan Conference Office, 1872), VI, 211-213; VII, 489-90.

One of the best-known Americans who first practiced the non-flesh-eating diet was Benjamin Franklin. After reading William Tryon's *Way to Health*, at the age of sixteen, Franklin determined to live the vegetarian diet. Economy was a major benefit, related the thrifty Franklin, but he also claimed "great clearness of head and quicker apprehension" as a result of his eating habits. Though he did not strictly follow this diet all of his life, he did at intervals and he considered it to be the better way of life. Franklin also realized that killing animals was "a kind of unprovoked murder," commenting that fish had never done "injury that might justify the slaughter" of the living creatures.[35]

An early American crusader for improved health was Sylvester Graham. After being ordained to the Presbyterian clergy, Graham became General Agent for the Pennsylvania State Society for the Suppression of the Use of Ardent Spirits. While engaged in this activity in 1829 he became acquainted with the Reverend William Metcalfe of the Bible Christian Church of Philadelphia. The Bible Christian Church had roots in England but had become a small independent congregation practicing vegetarianism as a tenet of faith.[36] Graham implemented Metcalfe's vegetarian ideal into the secular lecture field. Lecturing up and down the Atlantic coast, Graham preached the new diet and earned up to three hundred dollars per night in the process.[37]

Graham became a strong advocate of vegetarianism and its resultant improved health, which were of great interest to various social reformers and others interested in the welfare of mankind. Bronson Alcott's Brook Farm, the Oneida Community led by John Humphrey Noyes, and John

---

35 Benjamin Franklin, *The Autobiography of Benjamin Franklin* (New York: P. F. Collier and Son, 1909), 17, 35.

36 *History of the Philadelphia Bible Christian Church* (Philadelphia: J.P. Lippincott, 1922). See chapter 3 of this study.

37 Gerald Carson, *The Cornflake Crusade* (New York: Rinehart and Co., 1957), 46. *Graham's Science of Human Life* (Boston: Marsh Capen, Lyon and Webb, 1858) was a very influential work here and abroad.

Harvey Kellogg's Battle Creek Sanitarium all were influenced by Graham's doctrines of health.[38]

The educational reformer Amos Bronson Alcott, also influenced by Graham, founded a vegetarian cooperative society in 1843. In cooperation with Henry Wright, and Charles and William Lane, Alcott formed "Fruitlands" near Harvard, Massachusetts. One year later the colony had dissolved. Whereas Graham did not seem interested in the zoophilic aspects of vegetarianism, Alcott's group was. The concern for the welfare of animals went so far as to eliminate work for horses.[39]

The frontier of Kansas was the site of another colony of vegetarians in 1855. Led by Henry S. Clubb, later president of the Vegetarian Society of America, the Vegetarian Kansas Emigration Company started an "octagon settlement" near Fort Scott. The group had decided that animal flesh tends to injure the "physical, moral and intellectual" aspects of man. The settlement only had a short-lived existence of about one year with an undetermined number of settlers. The rigors of the Kansas seasons took its toll.[40]

There were a number of early publications advocating the vegetarian diet. Journals and magazines included W. A. Alcott's *Moral Reformer* in 1835, which was the first publication with a major interest in the vegetarian cause. Two short-lived publications of William Metcalfe propounded zoophilic reasons for the flesh-free diet: The *Independent Democrat* and the *Morning Star* in 1838. He followed these with the *Temperance Advocate* when that movement was peaking in the 1840s. The *Graham Journal* was also begun in 1838 by the Sylvester Graham contingent.

The above three leaders, Graham, Alcott, and Metcalfe, cooperated

---

38 Carson, 59.

39 Alice Felt Tyler, *Freedom's Ferment* (Minneapolis: University of Minnesota Press, 1944), 172-75.

40 Russell Hickman, "Vegetarian and Octagon Settlement Company," *Kansas Historical Quarterly*, II (November, 1933), 377-85.

in forming the Vegetarian Society, May 15, 1850, in New York City. Since that time there has been a sustained health movement by vegetarians in the United States and a resultant concern for animal life.[41]

The churches in America that have sponsored vegetarian precepts are the Bible Christian Church, the Shakers, and the Seventh-Day Adventists, all of which are discussed in detail later in this study.

For centuries theologians have taught that animals had a God-given right to live upon the earth and man had a moral obligation to avoid taking their life unnecessarily. The Hebrews of the Old Testament period cited biblical references for kindness to animals. The term *Tsa'ar ba'ale hayim* referred to the obligation Jews had to prevent cruelty to animals. Also included was the idea that God would hold man accountable for his actions toward animals.[42]

From Philo[43] to Aquinas[44] the accepted view was that animals had no rights and were for the use of man. When man's need for animals ceased, they would cease to exist. Grosseteste, Oxford University chancellor of the early thirteenth century, may have been an exception to this when he contended that all creatures will return to God.[45]

One of the earliest discussions of the possibility of animals having a soul was in 1967 by Pierre Bayle, French encyclopediest. In the article "Rorarius," Bayle goes into a lengthy discussion of the various historical and contemporary views pertaining to animals and their souls. Basically

---

41 "History of Vegetarianism in America," *The Vegetarian Messenger*, II (1851), 41-44; III (1852), 50-51, 79-80; Carson, 18-27.

42 Cohen, 47-57.

43 C.D. Yonge (trans.), *Works of Philo Judeaus* (London: Henry G. Bohn, 1854), I, 18-19; IV, 277-335.

44 Aquinas, 1024-25.

45 Anne Fremantle, *The Age of Belief* (New York: The New American Library, 1959), 133.

he rejects Descartes's soulless view and argues for the possibility that animals have a soul as eternal as man.[46]

Martin Luther, as mentioned previously, is reported to have told a young girl that in the "new heavens and a new earth...all creatures will not only be harmless, but lovely and joyful." Luther further asked rhetorically, "Why, then, should there not be little dogs in the new earth, whose skin might be as fair as gold, and their hair as bright as precious stones?" There is no evidence that Luther taught such ideas publicly.[47]

Joseph Butler, 1692-1752, Bishop of Durham, was one of the first clergymen to publicly advocate immortality of animals. Butler contended that "they should be immortal, and by consequence, capable of everlasting happiness." Speculating that animals may even "become rational and moral agents," Butler felt "we know not what latent powers and capacities they may be endued with."[48]

The Reverend John Hildrop issued a book entitled *Free Thought on the Brute Creation* in which he argued that before the fall of Adam animals were immortal. He further states that animals were created for God's glory and that God would not be wasteful and eliminate them. Hildrop held that animals will be recompensed with life eternal for their suffering upon the earth but that man should try to alleviate that suffering even now.[49]

Soame Jenyns, a follower of the humanitarian Earl of Saftsbury, published *Free Inquiry into the Nature and Origin of Evil* in 1757. Jenyns's had been influenced by the deist position that kindness should

---

46 Pierre Bayle, *Historical and Critical Dictionary* (Indianapolis: Bobbs and Merrill, 1965), 213-54.

47 Harwood, 145-46.

48 Joseph Butler, *The Analogy of Religion* (Philadelphia: J.B. Lippincott, 1882), 87-89.

49 John Hildrop, *Free Thoughts on the Brute Creation* (London: n.n., 1754); cited in Harwood, 149-51.

be tendered to all creatures and by an early interest in transmigration. Jenyns's final position was that God would ensure the immortality of animals as a simple matter of justice.[50]

Capel Berrow was another clergyman who followed Hildrop's teaching that animals had premortal spirits. They were very sinful, however, and so were cast down to earth in a very unpleasant position. Reverend Berrow taught that animals would have a chance to reform and, as man, would use this brief act of eternal existence to arrive at a more complete life.[51]

An Essay on the Future Life of Brute Creatures was written by Richard Dean in 1767. Dean wrote that animals suffered as a result of the Fall due to some fault of their own. Reveverend Dean argued that they would partake of the redemption and have "an endless Duration of Existence."[52]

The most famed advocate of animal immortality during the eighteenth century was John Wesley, founder of Methodism. Preaching "the whole animated creation" was subject to the fall of Adam, Wesley taught that "the golden chain" of creatures of God allowed animals and man to be "the offspring of one common Father." Preaching on the "great deliverance," Wesley put forth the concept that animals participated in the redemption of the Lord, which included "all that are capable of pleasure or pain, of happiness or misery." Indeed, man was to learn a lesson from this and "be tender of even meaner creatures, to show mercy to these also."[53] Wesley believed "something better remains after death for these poor creatures," and they "shall receive an ample

---

50 Harwood, 152-53.

51 Capel Berrow, *A Lapse of Souls in a State of Pre-Existence* (London, 1762); Cited in Harward, 153-55.

52 Harwood, 155-57.

53 John Wesley, *Sermons on Several Occasions* (New York: J. Soule and T. Mason, 1818), II, 113, 167-69.

amends for all their present sufferings."[54] Wesley's vegetarian practice, previously alluded to, for health benefits presumably, was connected with his concept that "on the new earth, no creature will kill, or hurt, or give pain to any other."[55]

Although some thinkers advocated the immortality of animal life, the majority of clerics and philosophers did not reply publicly to such unorthodox ideas. One of the few who responded was the Reverend Peter Browne. According to Browne, animals had sensitive perceptions but these were not because of any soul or thought process. He ridiculed the concept of animal immortality by saying that it was inconceivable that God would allow cheese weevils to flourish in heaven.[56]

The few spokesmen for animal immortality did not make a notable impression upon the established churches. It was not until after the Shakers and Latter-day Saints taught the concept that it was accepted by other groups as being quasi-official doctrine to be accepted by lay members. Among individuals in England who advocated an afterlife for animals was the Reveverend John G. Wood. Following a dearth of interest for almost a century, Wood published his belief that animals would obtain an eternal life. He felt most men were cruel to animals because they did not realize the truth of immortal life for animals.[57] Similarly, Earnest Bell explained in "*An Afterlife for Animals*" that it was only just and fair for animals to be rewarded after death.[58]

Frances Power Gobbe was a spokeswoman for the anti-vivisection movement in the late 1800s. Her arguments were based on sympathy for

---

54 Ibid., 123.

55 Ibid., 167.

56 Peter Browne, *Procedure, Extent, and Limits of Human Understanding* (London: n.n., 1729), 173; cited in Harwood, 148.

57 John G. Wood, *Man and Beast, Here and Hereafter* (London: n.n., 1874).

58 Earnest Bell, *An Afterlife for Animals* (London: Bell, n.d.).

pain caused to living creatures, on the belief animals would have an afterlife, and on her conviction that man's cruelty towards beasts would be condemned by God.[59]

The earliest American book devoted to zoophily for religious reasons was written by a medical doctor, E.D. Buckner. Buckner claimed that according to his knowledge, his was "the only work" published that considered "the immortality of animals from a biblical and philosophical hypothesis."[60] Buckner referred to the concept of "life potency, known as the soul, is immaterial and immortal and returns to God who gave it."[61] Critical of organized Christianity, Buckner felt by including animals his humanitarian ethic encompassed a wider scope of concern that most Christians ignored.

During the first half of the twentieth century most theologians and zoophilists ignored animal immortality until Agnes Carr wrote a small work concerning the eternal glory of animals after their redemption from death. Dedicated to "one of God's most understanding and loyal children," her dog, Bruce, Miss Carr stated:

> "The purpose of this work is to prove without question that what we have been pleased to call animals and birds, disdainfully and without concern, are in reality another people of God; that they have also been granted eternal life; that they are greatly honored in Heaven; that they assist in the judgment of the world; that in the new earth they are granted kingdoms of their own."[62]

Repeating a common complaint among members of humane

---

59 Frances Power Cobbe, *The Modern Rack* (London: S. Sonnenshein, 1889), 257-66.

60 Buckner, 12.

61 Ibid., 12-13.

62 Carr, 9.

societies, Carr was critical of traditional Christian churches when she stated "the churches must bear the terrible responsibility for their lack of interest in the dear silent creatures of God's household."[63]

It was in this setting that organized zoophily began in the United States, to which the Latter-day Saints made the greatest contribution of any Christian denomination to a theologically developed reverence for life.

---

63 Ibid.

Chapter 2

The Beginnings of Latter-day Saint Concern for Animals

The Church of Jesus Christ of Latter-day Saints, commonly known as the Latter-day Saints or "Mormons," are unique in their doctrine concerning animals. Throughout its history the leaders have very frequently advocated zoophily, based on man's responsibility to an eternal nature of animals.

The Latter-day Saint founder-prophet, Joseph Smith, first declared official doctrine on the use of animals in 1831. In response to a series of questions that Joseph Smith asked the Lord concerning the Shaker doctrines of Ann Lee about Christ's second appearing and marriage, Joseph Smith received a revelation known now as section 49 of the Doctrine and Covenants. Repeating the concept taught in Paul's first letter to Timothy concerning those who "forbiddeth to abstain from meats," Smith recorded that vegetarianism was not to be a tenet of the Latter-day Saints.[1] The revelation continued by stating that animals and birds were "ordained for the use of man for food and for raiment," even in abundance. Joseph Smith thus rejected the vegetarian doctrine later developed by the Shakers but concluded the section on the use of animals with the warning, "Wo be unto [the] man that sheddeth blood or

---

1 Doctrine and Covenants (Salt Lake City: The Church of Jesus Christ of Latter-day Saints, 1965) 49:18. See Timothy 4:3 concerning Paul's statement. No evidence of Shaker vegetarianism has been found prior to 1838. Perhaps some individual Shakers had proposed it but not leaders nor in discovered written form. Thus the 1831 question was coincidentally anticipatory of the Shaker practice.

that wasteth flesh and hath no need."[2]

An earlier effort at revising the Old Testament book of Genesis may have influenced the Latter-day founder on the use of animals. Whereas William Metcalfe of the Bible Christians altered the punctuation of Genesis 9:5, Joseph Smith greatly changed the verse by having it read: "And surely, blood shall not be shed, only for meat, to save your lives; and the blood of every beast will I require at your hands." The concept that man would be accountable to God for every animal he killed indicated animals were important to God and were not to be used by man indiscriminately. The phrase "to save your lives" limited the need for killing animals to the serious choice between human and animal life, in which case animal life was to be sacrificed to save mankind.

The next pronouncement pertaining to animals was also a result of the Prophet's work in revising the Bible by seeking revelation from God to answer questions concerning the wording of the text. Asking about the four beasts in Revelations 4:6, Joseph learned that

> they are figurative expressions, used by the Revelator, John, in describing heaven, the paradise of God, the happiness of man, and of beasts, and of creeping things, and of the fowls of the air; that which is spiritual being in the likeness of that which is temporal; and that which is temporal in the likeness of that which is spiritual; the spirit of man in the likeness of his person, as also the spirit of the beasts, and every other creature which God has created.[3]

In answering the question as to whether the beasts were individuals or were representatives of classes, God revealed that they were "limited to four individual beasts," shown to the Apostle John in vision to "represent the glory of the classes of beings in their destined order or

---

2 Doctrine and Covenants 49:19-21 (hereafter referred to as D&C).

3 D&C 77:2.

sphere of creation, in the enjoyment of their eternal felicity."[4] Within these passages of section 77:2-3 of the Doctrine and Covenants is found the basis of Mormon zoophily. Animals are given an eternal existence. In Latter-day Saint terminology this means animals have always existed in the past as spiritual beings in heaven before their existence on earth and will continue to exist after this mortal life.

In a revelation given to Joseph Smith concerning the creation of animals, the phrase attributed to God is to "let the earth bring forth the living creatures after his kind," which indicated a previous existence of animals of this "kind."[5] The revised account of the creation declared, "For I, the Lord God, created all things, of which I have spoken, spiritually before they were naturally upon the face of the earth." This proclaims a premortal existence of animals as well as humans.[6] It is also declared that "every beast of the field, and every fowl of the air...were also living souls."[7]

The Latter-day Saint leader taught that animals will be resurrected with bodies of flesh and bone restored to their premortal spirit body for an "eternal felicity." Their eternal state will be an improvement of this estate according to the Prophet, who stated that "they are full of knowledge" and will have power to move and act with greater facility than at present.[8]

An early Church newspaper, the *Times and Seasons*, published in Nauvoo, Illinois, during Joseph Smith's lifetime carried a doctrinal treatise which held that before the Fall "no ravenous beast sought for

---

4 D&C 77:3.

5 The Pearl of Great Price (Salt Lake City: The Church of Jesus Christ of Latter-day Saints, 1965), Moses 2:24.

6 Moses 3:5.

7 Moses 3:19.

8 D&C 77:4.

prey." In this condition "the lion ate vegetables like the ox" and "nothing did hurt nor destroy in all the Lord's holy mountain."[9] After describing the fallen condition of man and his environment a reference is made to Isaiah's descriptive prophecy of a restoration of the edenic condition. It is proclaimed that "wild beasts will become peaceable and harmless and eat vegetable food" again.[10] After quoting Isaiah's description of peaceful animals the writing summarized that "thus the beasts will cease to be ferocious, that the child can perform its wanderings among them unmolested."[11] The same publication in a later issue discussed the sparing use of animal flesh for food:

> Let man attend to these instructions, let them use the things ordained of God; let them be sparing of the life of animals; "It is pleasing saith the Lord that flesh be used only in times of winter, or of famine"—and why to be used in famine: because all domesticated animals would naturally die, and may as well be made use of by man, as not.[12]

During the annual conference of the Church in April 1843, Joseph Smith preached a sermon largely devoted to the discussion of beasts in the Bible, which was reported by Willard Richards and William Clayton. Stating the "grand secret was to show John what there was in heaven," Smith added, "God glorified Himself by saving all that His hands had made, whether beasts, fowls, fishes or men; and He will glorify Himself with them."[13] Referring specifically to the place of animals in the

---

9 "The Millennium," *Times and Seasons*, II (February 1, 1842), 274.

10 Ibid., 688.

11 Ibid., 689-90.

12 "The Word of Wisdom," *Times and Seasons*, III (June 1, 1842), 801.

13 Joseph Smith, *History of the Church of Jesus Christ of Latter-day Saints*, ed. B.H. Roberts (Salt Lake City: Deseret Book Co., 1959), V, 343. Hereafter

heavens after death, Joseph declared:

> Says one, "I cannot believe in the salvation of beasts." Any man who would tell you this could not be, would tell you that the revelations are not true. John heard the words of the beasts giving glory to God, and understood them. God who made the beasts could understand every language spoken by them. The four beasts were four of the most noble animals that filled the measure of their creation, and had been saved from other worlds, because they were perfect. They were like angels in their sphere, we are not told where they came from, and I do not know; but they were seen and heard by John praising and glorifying God."[14]

The actual beasts were considered God's creatures and were to be resurrected and glorified in His presence. But whenever the term *beast* was used figuratively in the Bible, the Prophet contended it was to refer to earthly kingdoms which had "degenerated, become corrupt, savage and beast-like." Animals were not used in the Bible to represent the kingdom of God or the Saints. They were not divine beings such as man and were definitely of an inferior nature to be ruled by man.[15]

In the summer of 1834 Joseph Smith taught more concerning man's relationship to animals on an expedition to Missouri. Known as "Zion's Camp" the group was led by the Prophet to Missouri to bring relief to the persecuted Saints in the state. A number of incidents are recorded concerning zoophily during this trek. After pitching tents one night, some of the men found and threatened to kill three rattlesnakes. Joseph commanded them not to hurt them and explained that the serpent will not lose its venom "while the servants of God possess the same

---

referred to as *HC*.

14 *HC*, V, 343-44.

15 Ibid., V, 341.

disposition."[16] Further he declared, "Men must become harmless before the brute creation" and then the animal kingdom will follow. He then exhorted them "not to kill a serpent, bird, or an animal of any kind" during the journey except to preserve themselves from starvation.[17]

Commenting that he had "frequently spoken on this subject" of kindness to animals and killing them only when necessary for food, the Prophet Joseph Smith attempted to determine if his followers had learned their lessons. On one occasion he found a group of his disciples watching a squirrel playing in a tree. Taking a gun, Smith shot the squirrel and walked off. When one of the brethren picked it up and said "We will cook this, that nothing may be lost," the teacher realized they had learned the lesson well.[18]

During the same trek to Missouri, this leader of the Church recorded in his history that when Hyrum Stratton and companion were making their bed one morning they found two rattlesnakes. Without making further doctrinal comment on the occasion he simply recorded that "they carefully carried [the snakes] out of the camp."[19]

Brigham Young acted as a captain during the expedition to Missouri, and when some men were going to kill a rattlesnake found in Young's tent, he exercised his authority and told them not to harm the snake. It is reported a Brother Carpenter took the snake "in his hands" and after taking it "beyond all danger" told the snake "not to return."[20]

The long journey from Kirtland, Ohio, to Jackson County, Missouri, brought many tensions. One personality conflict concerned Sylvester

---

16 Ibid., II, 71.

17 Ibid.

18 Ibid., II, 72.

19 Ibid., II, 101.

20 Ibid., II, 102.

Smith and his proposed treatment of a dog. While marching, as the story went, a dog had growled menacingly at Sylvester. Reportedly he had threatened, "If that dog bites me, I'll kill him."[21] Heber C. Kimball recorded that Joseph Smith turned to the angry Sylvester and said, "If you kill that dog, I'll whip you." The Prophet, according to Kimball, showed "the brethren how wicked and unchristian like such conduct appeared before the eyes of truth and justice."[22] Commenting further upon the incident, Joseph Smith said that men should be ashamed of such a spirit of contention and "ought never to place themselves on a level with the beasts; but be possessed of a more noble disposition."[23]

The 89th section of the Doctrine and Covenants contains the Latter-day Saint health code. Known as the Word of Wisdom, the Prophet Joseph Smith received the revelation on February 27, 1833. Containing prohibitions on the use of alcohol and tobacco, it also refers to the flesh of beasts and fowls. Advising the moderate or sparing use of flesh for food, the revelation told the Saints:

> Yea, flesh also of beasts and of the fowls of the air, I, the Lord, have ordained for the use of man with thanksgiving; nevertheless they are to be used sparingly.
>
> And it is pleasing unto me that they should not be used, only in times of winter, or of cold, or famine.
>
> All grain is ordained for the use of man and beasts, to be the staff of life, not only for man but for the beasts of the field, and the fowls of heaven, and all wild animals that run or creep on the earth;
>
> And these hath God made for the use of man only in times of famine and excess of hunger.[24]

---

21 Ibid., II, 83.

22 Ibid.

23 Ibid., II, 156.

24 D&C 89:12-15.

The Word of Wisdom precept definitely seems related to the previous concepts of Genesis 9:11 and Doctrine and Covenants 49:21 concerning the responsibility of man to not shed the blood of animals needlessly. The position of fish in the law of health to the Saints was referred to by a journalist on the Zion's Camp expedition. George A. Smith recalled Joseph Smith saying, "Fish was much healthier for us to eat than meat, and the use of fish in warm weather was not prohibited in the Word of Wisdom."[25]

Though some have advocated the sparing use of meat during the Church's existence, required vegetarianism is considered a false doctrine and has not been openly advocated by Church authorities.[26] When a serviceman wrote the Church asking a question about eating meat, he was answered by the Church publication for servicemen. The exchange was as follows:

> Q. Should we entirely abstain from eating meat in order to obey the Word of Wisdom?
>
> A. If you will note, the Word of Wisdom says that we are to eat meat sparingly. It does not ban it. It says, eat meat sparingly, and recommends that meat be eaten only in cold weather, or during times

---

25 George A. Smith, "My Journal," *The Instructor*, LXXXI (July, 1946), 323. The entry is dated July 22, 1834.

26 Presidents of the Church discussing vegetarianism are discussed in a later chapter. Another authority of the Church who has written supporting vegetarianism is Joseph F. Merrill in Conference Report, April 1948, 70-75. Also Joseph F. Merrill, *The Truth Seeker and Mormonism* (Independence, Mo.: Zion's Printing and Publishing Co., 1946), 247-62; and Joseph F. Merrill, Latter-day Saint Radio Addresses #17 and #18. Another apostle of the Church, John A. Widtsoe, gave support for vegetarianism in *The Word of Wisdom* (Salt Lake City: Deseret News Press, 1938), and in his *Joseph Smith* (Salt Lake City: Deseret Book Co., 1951), 202. Though both authors support it, neither specifically advocate Church practice of it.

of famine.[27]

Joseph Smith also referred to the millennial condition of the earth portrayed in Isaiah 11:6-9 and Doctrine and Covenants 65:25. The Doctrine and Covenants gives approval to Isaiah's teaching by stating, "In that day the enmity of man, and the enmity of beasts, yea the enmity of all flesh, shall cease from before my face."[28] This, of course, is in harmony with Joseph Smith's comments in relation to killing snakes earlier. A similar sentiment appeared in the Latter-day Saint newspaper from Kirtland, Ohio, which echoed Isaiah but specifically mentions the future abstinence of killing animals and eating flesh.

> "When these days come, every thing will be in its place. The beasts of the field, and the fowls of the air, instead of feeding upon flesh, will feed upon the herb and the grain, as was given them in the beginning. Then man will not shed the blood of his fellowman, nor beast the blood of its fellowbeast, nor fowl the blood of its fellow fowl but the Spirit of the Lord will be poured out upon all flesh, the curse be taken from off the earth, when it will again become an inheritance for the poor and the meek, when their [sic] will be peace thereon and good will towards man.[29]

---

27 *The Church News*: LDS Serviceman's Edition, No. 23, March 15, 1946, 8.

28 D&C 101:26.

29 *Evening and Morning Star*, II (June, 1833), 102.

Chapter 3

Brigham Young and Associates Concerning Animals

Latter-day Saints base their beliefs and practice not only on the written canons of the Church and the teachings of Joseph Smith, but also on pronouncements of subsequent Presidents of the Church. Each President has been considered a prophet and spokesman for God for the people of his day.[1] The issue of humanitarian treatment for animals was developed and presented by Joseph Smith, and Brigham Young further elucidated on the subject. Brigham Young, President of the Quorum of Twelve Apostles, succeeded Joseph Smith upon the latter's death in June 1844. During the next thirty-three years as leader of the Saints, Brigham Young frequently mentioned zoophilic and vegetarian principles. The place of animals in the economic life of pioneers was considered by President Young as well as the humanitarian aspects of kindness to animal life. As previously mentioned, Brigham Young had stopped the killing of a rattlesnake in favor of moving it unharmed.[2] This attitude was again evident in September 1845, when he spoke to the Nauvoo Legion saying "horses have feelings the same as he" and wanted "every man to be tender to his horse."[3]

---

1 Every word a prophet speaks is not binding. Joseph Smith taught that a prophet is a prophet only when he speaks as such. See *Teachings of the Living Prophets* ([Provo, Utah]: Brigham Young University Press, n.d.), 146-70.

2 Supra, 53.

3 Juanita Brooks, *On the Mormon Frontier: The Diary of Hosea Stout, 1844-1861* (Salt Lake City: University of Utah Press, 1964), 1, 67.

An early example of zoophily practiced by Brigham Young was an incident at Winter Quarters, Nebraska, during the trek west after the Latter-day Saints were driven from Nauvoo, Illinois. The story is that a man named Majors had asked Young if he should kill a mare that was felled by starvation and unable to get up. President Young is reported to have said, "No, never destroy life. Try to save her." An effort was put forth to spare the animal and the successful outcome recorded.[4]

Animals were even accorded the blessings of the priesthood by being administered to when ill by the sacred ritual of anointing with consecrated olive oil. Elders would lay their hands upon the head of the afflicted animal and a prayer would be offered that the beast be healed of its malady. In one instance the justification was that Joel had prophesied in the Old Testament that "in the latter days the Lord would pour out his spirit upon all flesh."[5] Since the horse qualified by having flesh, it was administered to by some priesthood holders and the result was that it "rolled twice over in great distress, sprang to his feet, squealed, vomited and purged, and the next morning was harnessed," able to pull a heavy load as usual.[6] Another account recalled that a sick mare belonging to a Brother U. Perk was treated by drenching and after having "laid on hands she felt easier."[7]

During the exodus to the Rocky Mountains Brigham Young gave advice to the pioneering Saints on their hunting habits. One diarist

---

4 John R. Young, *Memoirs of John R. Young* (Salt Lake City: Deseret News, 1920), 48.

5 Joel 2:28.

6 Elden Watson (ed.), *Manuscript History of Brigham Young, 1846-1847* (Salt Lake City: Elden Watson, 1971), 84. Also see Preston Nibley, *Presidents of the Church* (Salt Lake City: Deseret Book Co., 1959), 235, concerning Hyrum Smith's widow and her oxen.

7 "Autobiography of J.D. McAllister," typed manuscripts in Brigham Young University Library, Provo, Utah, II, 125.

records that Brigham "reproved" the people for "running after the Buffalo."[8] Another journalist, a brother of Brigham, Lorenzo Dow Young, reported, "No game was allowed to be killed except as it was wanted for food."[9] Hosea Stout complained however, that "the hunting fever seized upon the brethren" and "regardless of previous arraingements [sic]" had often ran and left their responsibilities and went "shooting at buffalo all day." Stout complained that "many were killed and left but few brought into camp."[10]

Because zoophily has not been a cardinal principle of the Church, many members have been avid hunters throughout the Church's history though no printed sermons of authorities have advocated it, indeed, as the thesis of this study attempts to show, they have generally been zoophilic in principle. In numerous sermons delivered in Utah during his tenure as President of The Church of Jesus Christ of Latter-day Saints, Brigham Young frequently mentioned animals. On one such occasion he taught, "If we maltreat our animals, or each other, the spirit within us, our traditions, and the Bible, all agree in declaring it is wrong."[11]

The principle behind Young's zoophilic tendencies are found in his sermons as being related to man's responsibility for bringing about peace with animals and preparing for the millennial reign pictured by Isaiah. For example, Young held that the people should be holy and then the earth would follow and be holy as well. If mankind was filled with the Spirit of God and was peaceful, according to President Young, then all animal life would also be filled with peace. He taught that "the more

---

8 Brooks, I, 317.

9 Lorenzo Dow Young, "Biography of Lorenzo Dow Young," Utah Historical Quarterly, XIV (1947), 84.

10 Brooks, I, 316-17.

11 George D. Watt, et al. (reporters), *Journal of Discourses* (Liverpool: Latter-day Saint Book Depot, 1854), I, 337. Hereafter referred to as *JD*.

kind we are to our animals, the more will peace increase and the savage nature of the brute creation will vanish away."[12] Young claimed it was man's fault strife existed on the earth and it was therefore up to man to "remove the foul blot." In order to "restore all things to their primeval purity and innocence" man must have the help of God and live His laws. Bringing it to a personal level, Young argued that "each people belonging to the human family" has a responsibility in "removing the curse" from all creatures on earth.[13] As for himself, Brigham Young stated if he saw an animal in the mud he made it his business to stop and help get it out.[14] Even the lowly grasshopper was not driven from the garden of Brigham Young, but rather he would say they were welcome, "these creatures of God."[15]

Many of Brigham Young's sermons dealt with the practical problems of pioneer life. In this vein were his remarks concerning the care of livestock raised by the Mormon pioneers. This interest represented economic concern as well as consideration for the animal suffering. For example, Young preached that the way sheep were being treated was "by no means conducive to their thrift." He exhorted the Church members to protect the sheep from wolves, dogs, and inexperienced herd boys. President Young complained that often sheep were huddled too close in filthy pens for too long a period of time, and "for this you will be called to judgment," he warned.[16] Later, the

---

12 *JD*, I, 203.

13 *JD*, X, 301-302.

14 *JD*, X, 296.

15 *JD*, XII, 121. The famed cricket episode of 1848 points up the practical aspects of the zoophilic doctrine that when man's existence is at stake the rest of creation is to be subjected to control. Even then the gulls, more than man, were the successful means of bringing a proper balance to nature.

16 *JD*, X, 201-202.

President-prophet said the Latter-day Saints would "never inherit the Celestial kingdom" until they learned to take proper care of the things entrusted to them on this earth by the Lord. Specifically referring to livestock, Young said the people should "take care of their cattle and horses," and he who did not would "lay himself liable to censure in the eyes of justice."[17] Neglecting livestock was "a grievous sin," according to Young. Many people treated animals "as nought" and allowed them to become "diseased and sickly."[18] It was ironic that a shipload of Brigham Young's cattle going to market in Chicago during the 1870s was widely publicized and helped lead to better transportation laws for animal shipments.[19]

If animals or birds seemed to jeopardize man's position, however, President Young did not avoid action. Hosea Stout records that John Pack and John D. Lee each led a party of one hundred hunters which sought to eradicate the overpopulated and pestilent "crows and other noxious varmin." A banquet was to be provided the winning team killing the most predators by the team killing the least. Stout declined his invitation to join the hunt by commenting that he was "not feeling very war-like" at the time.[20] Stout also recorded the action of the Deseret

---

17 *JD*, XI, 141.

18 *JD*, XII, 218.

19 Emily Stewart Leavitt, *Animals and Their Legal Rights* (New York: Animal Welfare Institute, 1968), 30.

20 Stout, II, 338. John D. Lee said that the Council of Fifty (a governing body in the Territory) organized the hunt due to the "wasters and destroyers" naming, "wolves, wildcats, catamounts, pole cats, minks, Bear, Panthers, Eagles, Hawks, owls, crow or Ravens and Magpies." These, according to Lee, were "very numberous [sic]...troublesome" and destructive. It was estimated that "1,000's of dollars worth of grain and stock have already been destroyed." Brigham Young was credited with nominating Lee and Pack to "carry on a war of extermination against the above named wasters and destroyers." In Robert G. Cleland and Juanita Brooks, *A Mormon Chronicle: The Diary of John D.*

legislature concerning zoophily. The legislative act on "cruel treatment to domestic animals [was] read and passed" in 1852.[21]

Concerning the health aspects of eating meat, Brigham Young commented frequently. He preached that "a thorough reformation is needed in regard to our eating." The prophet said if the people were willing to listen to the words of God "they will cease eating swine's flesh."[22] Pork was rejected by Young in favor of bread, milk, and eggs for the breakfast of pioneer children.[23] More frequently Young attacked meat eating in general. Preaching that "flesh should be used sparingly, in famine and in cold," the President of the Church told the women to "stop your children from eating meat, and especially fat meat."[24] Rather the children were to eat vegetables and wholesome bread.[25]

Brigham Young felt affluence was taking its toll among the Saints. As the pioneers prospered they began to indulge in too much "sweet cake, plum pudding, roast beef and so on," and this was the cause of increased disease among the Saints.[26] Describing a visit to the homes of the pioneers he claimed to find beef, pork, and other luxuries "so as to shorten their days and the days of their children."[27] If they would eat more properly, Young claimed, they would "lay the foundation for

---

Lee, 1948-1876 (San Marino: Huntington Library, 1955), I, 82.

21 Stout, II, 429.

22 *JD*, XII, 192-193.

23 *JD*, XII, 201-203.

24 *JD*, XII, 209.

25 *JD*, XIX, 68.

26 *JD*, XIX, 67.

27 *JD*, XIII, 142.

longevity" and even live "hundreds of years."[28] Rather than living on "beef, pork, mutton, sweet meats," and other unhealthy foods, those who would live long would "live as our first parents did on fruits."[29]

Next to the scriptures, the most important pronouncements from prophets to the Latter-day Saints are statements signed by the First Presidency of the Church. During Brigham Young's term as President two such statements contained references to animals. The first was written "To the Saints in Utah" by Brigham Young and his two counselors, Heber C. Kimball and Jedediah M. Grant. It was dated September 14, 1854, and referred to people with a cantankerous attitude. They claimed that such "a person becomes disagreeable to himself, to his family...to his animals for they have reason, and in short to all the true intelligences around him."[30]

The second statement was signed by Brigham Young and a new pair of counselors, George A. Smith and Daniel H. Wells. Concerning those living a new type of economic order, the official statement gave advice to provide adequate food and shelter for "humanely caring for stock during winter."[31]

Others followed President Brigham Young's concern, as is evidenced by his counselors Jedediah Grant and Heber C. Kimball. Grant claimed that he "never misuse[d] a beast."[32] He declared in a sermon that people who "beat, and kick, and pound their cattle, horses"

---

28 *JD*, XII, 37.

29 Ibid.

30 James R. Clark, ed., *Messages of the First Presidency* (Salt Lake City: Bookcraft, 1965), II, 150.

31 Ibid., 262-63.

32 *JD*, II, 73.

are exhibiting "nonsense."[33] He then declared: "Do right, be kind and gentle."[34] Grant recalled as a young boy his brother had asked if there were quails in heaven. Jedediah meditated on the subject and felt there was a positive answer. He read John Wesley's views on animal life in heaven and was confirmed in his convictions. Upon joining the Mormons, Grant read Joseph Smith's views in the Doctrine and Covenants and said the teaching of animals existing in the hereafter gave him "great joy and satisfaction."[35]

Heber C. Kimball spent some time in a sermon of 1857 to chastise those in the community who used spurs on their horses. He contended a decent horse was "as good as we are in their sphere of action; they honour their calling," adding that men "do not, when we abuse them."[36] Kimball taught that animals were being abused, and in an impassioned plea called for a halt to current cruelty. "We have our Spanish fixings—a pair of spurs that will weigh seven pounds, ringing and gingling as though all hell was coming. Why don't you put them away? I want you to make an ox goad with a spike in the end of it, and ram that into your horse, and get this instead of spurs, and destroy a horse at once. I cannot keep a decent horse, neither can Brother Brigham, or any other man; for the boys will kill them. Let them rest: they are as good as we are in their sphere of action; they honour their calling, and we do not, when we abuse them: they have the same life in them that you have, and we should not hurt them. It hurts them to whip them, as bad as it does you; and when they are drawing as though their daylights would fly out of them, you must whip, whip, whip. Is there religion in that? No; it is

33 Ibid.

34 Ibid.

35 *JD*, III: 8.

36 *JD*, V, 137-38.

an abuse of God's creation that he has created for us."[37]

Kimball continued by observing that most people did not believe in the resurrection of animals. To support his view that animals do live a celestial life he referred to Elijah's vision of horses pulling war chariots. Asking, "Where did they come from?" he answered his own question by referring to the doctrine of eternal existence for animal life and stated they were "created before" in heaven.[38] Concluding his remarks on animals, Kimball admonished all to "let us be merciful to the brute creation."[39]

Counselor Kimball felt "a man that is abusive to his animal is apt to be the same to his wife or child." He explained the spirit of love would never kill or destroy unnecessarily.[40] Further, he declared the spirit of the Lord was needed to show kindness to the animal world.[41] Kimball also supported President Brigham Young concerning the eating of pork, saying "pig meat is not good."[42]

A story relating to Heber C. Kimball's concern for animals was told to the general Sunday School conference of the Latter-day Saints in an effort to motivate Church members to be more humane in their treatment of animals. Kimball reportedly was walking down a Salt Lake City street when he viewed a man abusing a horse. Turning to his companions Kimball said, "That horse will demand justice of that man some time and

---

37 Ibid.

38 Ibid.

39 Ibid.

40 *JD*, VI, 128-29.

41 *JD*, IX, 336.

42 *JD*, XII, 190-91.

will get it."[43]

Orson Hyde, an apostle under Brigham Young, claimed he would be mortified if he were to allow his livestock to die because of neglect. He expressed his desire that the Saints would not be "the authors of misery to any part of creation."[44] Similarly, apostle Franklin D. Richards advised members of the Church in the famed Salt Lake Tabernacle to take their religion to the canyons. It would help the "cattle be more kindly." Treating animals with love, they would not beat them so much and the cattle would respond with more work.[45]

The intellectual Orson Pratt, also a member of the Quorum of Twelve, discoursed frequently on the state of animals in mortality and in eternity. In comparing man and animals Pratt emphasized the vast difference in mental powers. He pointed out that man "is advanced far beyond the apparent manifestations of knowledge that exist among the lower order of beings."[46] He stated that there exists only "small glimmerings of light" in the brute creation. He did admit, however, that animals "have some degree of information and knowledge that man is not in possession of."[47] Though some of this was regarded as the instincts of animals, Pratt did point out that the behavior of animals during Noah's day and the Biblical account of the Flood was quite unusual in that the animals' behavior exhibited more than instinct. Pratt commented:

> The beasts of the field—that appeared to have more inspiration than

---

43 Conference Report (April, 1899), 76-77.

44 *JD*, XI, 150. Hyde did not show much concern in *JD*, V, 356-357, or XVII, 7, however.

45 *JD*, V, 47.

46 *JD*, III, 97-98.

47 Ibid.

> the men and women of that age, began to come from the forests towards the ark, and finally the door was closed. They must have been prophetic beasts, beasts that had revelations, beasts that were able to judge far better than the world of mankind in that age.[48]

The millennial conditions of animals was described by Orson Pratt in a sermon near the end of his life. Following the theme of Isaiah, Pratt said the enmity between beasts would cease and no longer would they "prey devouring and feasting upon another."[49] The change would occur at the Second Coming of Jesus Christ, according to Pratt. It would not be a change to immortality for animals, but rather "a change sufficient to alter the ferocious nature of beasts, birds and fishes."[50] Commenting on the gentle, harmless nature of lions and serpents during the millennium, Pratt reminded his hearers that "animals did not devour one another until after the fall, neither was there any death."[51] Answering the question of what animals ate in the Garden of Eden, he replied, "The grass, and the herbs, and every green thing were their feed."[52] After stating that the millennial reign would be a restoration of the peaceful condition of Eden, Pratt said that the animal creation "will manifest more intelligence and more knowledge than they do now."[53] One characteristic to be bestowed on animals during the millennial state will be that of language. Pratt used scriptural texts to support his view that

---

48 *JD*, XXI, 174-75.

49 *JD*, XX, 18.

50 Ibid.

51 Ibid.

52 Ibid.

53 Ibid.

animals would have a language of praise.[54]

One early leader in the Church, Luke Johnson, represented what was more typically the traits of men on the frontier. Rattlesnakes in particular did not receive kind treatment by Luke Johnson, as Brigham Young and Joseph Smith would have desired. On the occasions recorded, however, Johnson did justify his killing of rattlesnakes by using them for medicinal oil.[55]

On the other extreme, Parley P. Pratt, brother to Orson and member of the Council of the Twelve, referred to animal life in a vegetarian context. He commented on the Genesis creation account by saying that "flesh and blood were never sanctioned to glut their souls or gratify" men's appetites.[56]

George A. Smith, counselor to Brigham Young, felt inclined to take the whip to a man who was abusing his defenseless oxen. Smith maintained, "Every man in Israel is responsible as to how he uses his cattle."[57] He further declared that when he was in charge of emigrant trains he used "extra exertion" to prevent cruelty to the animals.[58]

That the Mormon pioneers were generally kind to their animals is attested to by Colonel Thomas L. Kane. A non-Mormon, Kane had befriended the persecuted Saints and pleaded their cause to the federal government during the days of Joseph Smith and Brigham Young. A

---

54 Ibid.

55 Paul Dahl, ed., *Journal of William Clayton* (Provo, Utah: Grant Stevenson, 1964), 108. Also see Andrew Jenson, "Day by Day with the Utah Pioneers," *Deseret News* [Salt Lake City], May 23, 1947; April 28, 1947.

56 Parley P. Pratt, *Voice of Warning* (Independence, Mo.: Zion's Printing and Publishing Co., 1928), 91.

57 *JD*, II, 367.

58 Ibid.

close friend of Brigham Young, Kane was impressed with a "strong trait" of the Mormons being "their kindness to their brute dependents, and particularly to their beasts of draught."[59] Kane recalled the Latter-day Saint pioneers had given the animals a Sabbath holiday and expressed his personal belief that they would have washed the horses with wine, if they had any, they exhibited such concern for the animals.[60]

It is thus seen that during the formative years of the Latter-day Saint doctrine, many leaders and others were teaching the humane treatment of animals. The leaders were looked upon as prophets, seers, and revelators of the Lord's will to the world, and the consistent theme never varies with respect to zoophily. They taught that men would be accountable for their actions towards animals, the future resurrected glory in heaven of animals, and the admonition to eat animal flesh "sparingly."

---

59 William Mulder and Russell Mortenson, *Among the Mormons* (New York: Alfred A. Knopf, 1958), 205.

60 Ibid.

Chapter 4

George Q. Cannon: Advocate of Kindness to Animals

Unlike other Christian denominations in America, the Latter-day Saints have continually stressed zoophily. During the second half of its first century the Church began to establish programs for the promotion of zoophily among its members. Via the printed page, George Q. Cannon was the prime motivator for these programs during the presidencies of John Taylor and Wilford Woodruff.

John Taylor, an Englishman converted to the Latter-day Saint faith in Canada, became President of the Church after the death of Brigham Young. No written evidence has been discovered indicating President Taylor, nor his successor Wilford Woodruff, publicly advocated zoophily or vegetarianism. During this period, however, much was being written by George Q. Cannon, a Church leader and first counselor in the First Presidency to both John Taylor and Wilford Woodruff, and later to Lorenzo Snow. Cannon was editor of the *Juvenile Instructor*. Though President Cannon was owner and publisher of the *Juvenile Instructor*, it was meant to be, and served the role as, the official organ of the fledgling Sunday School organization of The Church of Jesus Christ of Latter-day Saints. Begun in 1866, Cannon served as its editor the rest of the nineteenth century.[1]

The first zoophilic editorial written by Cannon was in the *Juvenile Instructor* for September, 1868. It was typical of many written by President Cannon which followed through the turn of the century. The

---

1 Marba C. Josephson, "George Q. Cannon," *The Instructor*, LXXXIV (February, 1949), 52-55, 89; and J.N. Washburn, "Capsule History of the Sunday School," *The Instructor*, LXXXIV (December, 1949), 649-55.

editor's concern was youthful cruelty to animals and developing into a tendency of cruelty to humans. But George Q. Cannon also expressed concern for the animal for its own sake. One paragraph of this first editorial was an example of the zoophilic concern evident throughout the last quarter of the nineteenth century in the Church. Cannon wrote:

> No man or woman, no boy or girl, who has any kind feelings will inflict unnecessary pain upon any creature. Such persons will not hurt a worm. Animals feel pain very acutely. They know when they are treated kindly and when they are abused. God has given them this feeling, and if men or boys abuse them, He will condemn and punish them for so doing. They prove themselves unworthy of the power they have, and, by their cruelty, they sink beneath the brute.[2]

Commenting on the cruelty of some children, Cannon mentioned the practices he abhorred. They included sticking pins in flies and pulling off their wings, cutting ears off cats and drowning them, beating animals, spurring horses until the blood ran, and exhibiting a general lack of feeling for animal life. Analyzing such behavior, Cannon contended that such a boy "will likely grow up to be a cruel, unfeeling, hard-hearted man." He also felt cruel boys were in reality cowards, cruelly dominating weaker beings but cringing before stronger ones. Concluding his first editorial on the subject of cruelty to animals, Cannon admonished all children to "remember these words, do not hurt anything unnecessarily." If a boy were cruel it would "serve the boy perfectly right if some man were to give him a sound thrashing," and thus help him learn "how to sympathize with the poor brute whom he had mistreated."[3]

The next editorial was a very lengthy one and was prompted by a cattle drive in Salt Lake City and environs witnessed by editor Cannon.

---

2 George Q. Cannon, "Editorial Thoughts," *The Juvenile Instructor*, III (September 1, 1868), 132. Hereafter referred to as *JI*.

3 Ibid.

He described a problem concerning horses, of which "large numbers" were brought into the city. Cannon explained that the only successful technique to catch the wild horses was by the lasso rope. But, he said, "this is a very cruel way of catching horses, and ought never to be practiced by people like us."[4] President Cannon contended that lassoing horses was "fit only for savages" and a "rude, barbarous people, like the Californians were when we settled this valley."[5] The practice was further criticized in the editorial because the horses were "ruined" by the operation. The use of spurs on the horses was also condemned because it was "very cruel." Expressing disgust with the use of spurs, George Q. Cannon stated, "They treated the poor dumb creatures, which God had given them as though they had no feeling."[6] "Such conduct is brutal and sinful," the editorial continued, "and punishment in some form will fall upon those who indulge in it."[7] Further developing the concept that man would be held accountable by God for his treatment of animals, Cannon said cruelty to animals was "very sinful." He asked the question, "Will a man who has the Spirit of God be cruel or unkind to dumb creatures because they are in his power?" He answered with an emphatic "No." Indeed, he wrote, "the spirit of God fills men and boys with love and compassion" and thus they would no sooner hurt an animal than they would a human companion.[8]

Warning the young ladies about such cruel men, George Q. Cannon told them:

"Young ladies, never put yourselves in the power or under the

---

4 *JI*, VI, (May 13, 1871), 76.

5 Ibid.

6 Ibid.

7 Ibid.

8 Ibid.

> control of young men who treat their animals badly; for if you become their wives, they will abuse you. A man who is cruel to a helpless, dumb creature like a horse or an ox, which cannot complain of him, has cruelty in his nature; and when he gets a child or a woman in his power, he will be unkind to her; he is not fit to be a husband or a father, and ought to be shunned."[9]

The theme of cruelty to animals indicating a cruel trait that would be manifest in a man's treatment of humans was frequently expressed by Cannon as editor of the *Juvenile Instructor*. Elder Cannon emphasized judgment by God in the same editorial when he commented that God had made the beasts and put men in charge of them. Thus, Cannon reasoned, God would "call us to judgment for all our acts" in relation to animals. If man was cruel to animals it indicated he was "a coward and a tyrant." As a result of man's misuse of his power over animals, it would be taken from him in the hereafter. On the other hand, Cannon proposed, if man exercised his power over animals with kindness, more power would be given to him after the resurrection.[10] The editorial advocate for kindness to animals suggested men decide how they would like to be treated by others who held power over them, and then to treat animals as they would have themselves treated. He expressed his sentiments with the phrase, "Be kind, therefore, to all the creatures around."[11]

The New York Society for the Prevention of Cruelty to Animals received favorable comment from editor Cannon in a front page editorial on December 8, 1873. To describe the definition of "humane" the editor used an engraving depicting a humane officer and an officer of the law requesting a farmer to allow a calf to relieve a bursting udder on a cow. Elder Cannon admonished his readers to think about their treatment of animals with the advice to "just stop long enough to ask yourselves the

---

9 Ibid.

10 Ibid.

11 Ibid.

question: would it be humane?"[12] Following the lead editorial was a story concerning a dog being mistreated by a young boy. A man stopped the boy from further cruelty and gave the advice to "never treat another, whether human being or dumb animal, as you would not like to be treated yourself." A third article on the editorial page told of a wounded water buffalo gaining revenge on the hunter, and though no mention of cruelty was made, neither was there any indication of needed revenge to the buffalo.[13]

President Cannon suggested the need for organizing a branch of the Society for the Prevention of Cruelty to Animals in Utah in an editorial of 1874. After commenting on the un-Godlike cruelty to animals as a general principle, he related two specific examples found in Utah: pigeon shooting contests and the neglect of horses. Pigeon shooting as a sport, according to Cannon, was "a mockery." Cannon sympathized with the pigeons that were "mangled, mutilated, with backs broken, limbs fractured, flesh torn and every nerve quivering with pain."[14] He felt there was nothing ennobling in subjecting birds to such pain and suffering in the name of sport and that men should be more humane to members of the bird kingdom.

The editor of the *Juvenile Instructor* painted a word picture of how some young men were cruel to their horses. The young man of his example rode a horse to a party in a neighboring community. Anxious to get to the party, the horse was driven "furiously" five to ten miles. After arriving at the party the young man left the sweating horse unattended in a "freezing wind or biting snow storm for six or seven hours."[15] The party was over, the youth rode the horse home as fast as possible. Upon reaching home in the wee hours of the morning, the

---

12 *JI*, VIII (December 20, 1873), 201-2.

13 Ibid., 205.

14 *JI*, IX (December 5, 1874), 294.

15 Ibid.

horse was again left unattended so the youth could retire to bed as quickly as possible. Cannon elaborated on the cruelty man showed to his animals and by the lack of responsibility shown to the animals entrusted to man by God. Reference was made to the sparing of cattle in Nineveh and the Mosaic law which granted protection to the corn-treading ox.

After making the initial effort towards humane treatment to animals in the *Juvenile Instructor* President Cannon printed contributions by other writers on the subject of zoophily. The killing of a porcupine by two young boys prompted the concerned pen of one contributor to the magazine. Because the boys had "cruelly taken a life which they could not restore" the humanitarian writer suggested punishment. He claimed that men were to be judged according to deeds done in the body, which included being "cruel to any dumb unoffensive animal."[16]

Another contributor of humanitarianism, J. H. Parry, quoted Isaiah 11:6 concerning the wolf dwelling peacefully with the lamb. Parry stated that the animal world was at peace before sin entered the world with the fall of Adam and Eve. He contended that much was to "be done to educate mankind to acts of love and kindness" before the millennial state would bring back the condition of love and harmony with the brute creation.[17] Because man was "the first who sinned," man was to "take the first step towards restoring the earth to its primeval state of happiness."[18] First man must "learn to be kind to the animal creation" about them, wrote Parry, and then the animals would reciprocate. Commenting specifically about the snake, Parry said that men seem to desire to kill snakes immediately at the sight of them. But, he wrote, all animals contain "a certain degree of intelligence," therefore they deserve kind treatment.[19] He wrote that "kindness to the animal creation is

---

16 E. H., "Reflections," *JI*, X (January, 1875), 9.

17 J. H. Parry, "Kindness to Animals," *JI*, XV (January, 1880), 2.

18 Ibid.

19 Ibid.

aprinciple of the gospel we have to learn."[20] Indeed, thought Parry, it was to be the efforts of the Saints in living the principles of kindness that would bring about the millennial reign of peace spoken of by the prophet Isaiah.

"Don't kill the birds, our Heavenly Father made them," pled another article George Q. Cannon accepted for the Sunday School publication. After discussing the beauty and utility of birds, the writer stated how "thoughtless and cruel are those who would hurt or destroy any of God's creatures."[21] He requested that boys "remember that it is wrong to take the life of anything needlessly."[22] He concluded with a plea for all to live the "Golden Rule" at all times.

James Hardy contributed an article on kindness to animals to the *Juvenile Instructor* while George Q. Cannon was the editor. Hardy stated that men were "taught to be kind and merciful to our dumb animals by the will of God."[23] Citing many Old Testament references of kindness to animals, he also recalled the New Testament references to God's "providential care" for birds. He concluded his short comment on animals with the remark that it was "mankind's duty to be kind to these inferior animals."[24]

George Q. Cannon resumed personal involvement in articles concerning humane treatment of animals with a short story about a girl and her pet cat. Elder Cannon described the girl as one "fond of dumb creatures" and who never ill-treated them. The front page story praised

---

20 Ibid., 3.

21 G. M., "Don't Kill the Birds!" *JI*, XV (June 15, 1880), 137.

22 Ibid.

23 James Hardy, "Kindness to Animals," *JI*, XV (April 15,1880), 88.

24 Ibid.

children who did not "delight in giving pain to others."[25]

Editorially, President Cannon continued to write on zoophilic topics. One editorial decried the "far too general" disposition of Latter-day Saints to "kill wild animals and birds, and every insect which crosses their path."[26] He asked, "Why there should be such eagerness to kill these creatures." If men hunted game "because they have pleasure in taking their lives," President Cannon suggested the hunter imagine himself in the position of the hunted. The editor admitted a "great difference between animals and human beings," but declared all were given life by God and so should be respected and treated with kindness. Animals were meant to be used by man for food, according to Cannon, but only with "prudence and thanksgiving and not wastefully."[27] He contended that too often animals' lives were "very much wasted to gratify the hunting propensity of some men."[28] He explained that if humans needed animals for food the "Lord is not displeased if they kill it." On the other hand, Cannon emphasized, if people hunted for the "mere pleasure of killing" then sin was committed.[29] Cannon then referred to prophecies concerning the time when "wild and ferocious" animals would dwell together in kindness. But, Cannon warned, before that day would come, men must "cease their war upon the animals, the reptiles and the insects." In the peaceful state looked for in the future, Cannon promised that animals would be harmless and "universal peace will prevail."[30]

---

25 *JI*, XVI (September 1, 1881), 193.

26 *JI*, XXIV (December 1, 1889), 548.

27 Ibid.

28 Ibid.

29 Ibid., 549.

30 Ibid.

An editorial against killing began by referring to the "sacredness of human life."[31] Self-defense, according to Cannon, was the only reason warranting the taking of human life. Animal life was then considered by the editorialist. Children, wrote Cannon, should be impressed with the value of animal life. The reason given by President Cannon for the training of children was a common theme with him. He argued that those who hunt for the "mere pleasure of killing" would develop a "feeling of indifference" to suffering. People who were indifferent to the pain of animals, concluded Cannon, would "more likely...use their weapons against their fellow-creatures" when provoked to anger.[32] He stated that God had given animals to man for man's sustenance, but animals were "not to be wasted, not to be killed for sport," and "not to be exterminated from the face of the earth."[33] Man would be held accountable to God for his treatment of animals, wrote Elder Cannon. Finally, the editorial summarized, the millennial reign of peace between man and animals would come.

To bring about the millennium, Cannon reiterated, "man should set the example" and cease to "hunt and destroy." Cannon speculated that if man would control his "destructive propensities" a different spirit might "take possession of fowls, animals, fish, reptiles and insects." In this fashion, Cannon theorized, peace may come and animals would be helpful friends to mankind.[34]

Birds were the special object of George Q. Cannon's concern in an editorial of 1893. Specifically condemned by Elder Cannon was the plumage used in ladies' hats. He wrote that "a fashion of this character

---

31 *JI*, XXVI (July 15, 1891), 442-43.

32 Ibid.

33 Ibid.

34 Ibid., 444.

should not prevail among us."[35] He argued that no girl should "adorn herself with feathers obtained from the slaughter of birds." Cannon wrote that neither "mere amusement" nor "gratification of vanity" were proper excuses for killing birds and animals. Cannon advised parents to teach their boys that it was "wicked to take the life even of the humblest animals or the most insignificant bird," emphasizing that such a practice was "murderous."[36]

Announcement of a special "Humane Day" to be observed in the Sunday Schools of The Church of Jesus Christ of Latter-day Saints was made in the *Juvenile Instructor* of January, 1897.[37] As editor, George Q. Cannon commented on the occasion. He felt it was very appropriate that the Church Sunday Schools teach kindness to animals as the public schools did not pay sufficient attention to such "moral duties." The children of the Sunday School could learn the principle of kindness through the medium of their pets. Stressing the importance of the new Humane Day, Cannon stated:

> There can be no doubt in the mind of any person who believes in the God of heaven that He will hold man accountable for any ill treatment of the creatures He has placed under his control, and those who misuse or treat them with cruelty will be called to an account for such acts. It is not our acts to our fellow man alone that we shall be called to an account for, but our acts to the creations of our Father in heaven. These animals are His, He created them, and they are not outside of the reach of His love and care, and they cannot be badly treated with impunity. This is the lesson that should be impressed deeply upon the minds of the young, and when they are awakened to realize this they will be more humane to the animals they have in their keeping and be more likely to treat them with consideration and

---

35 *JI*, XXVIII (November 15, 1893), 712-13.

36 Ibid.

37 *JI*, XXIX (January 15, 1897), 58-60.

kindness.[38]

One year after the first Humane Day the general superintendency of the Sunday School, composed of George Q. Cannon, superintendent, and counselors George Goddard and Karl G. Maeser, spoke of the day as "Mercy Day."[39] The purpose of the day, according the superintendency, was to "inspire in the hearts of our young people a love for all the creations of our Heavenly Father" because "He commands kindness and consideration in their behalf."[40] Scriptural references were given to the readers for aid in presenting the principle of mercy to animals. The article closed with a favorable report of the treatment of animals in India.

The second anniversary of Humane Day was noted in the *Juvenile Instructor* with a lengthy article on George T. Angell, founder of the American Humane Education Society, the Massachusetts Society for the Prevention of Cruelty to Animals, and the American Band of Mercy. Mention was also made of his publication, *Our Dumb Animals*, which frequently was the source of stories used in the *Juvenile Instructor* that pertained to animals.[41]

George Q. Cannon added thoughts of animal communication in one of his last editorials on the subject of animals. Because animals could not clearly express their pain to man, Cannon theorized, men were frequently thoughtless in their treatment of the brute creation. Kind concern for animal welfare would bring forth expressions of gratitude from the animals if they could speak to man, he stated. One act of kindness proposed by Cannon in the same editorial was for Church congregations to build a shelter at the meetinghouse for the animals used

---

38 Ibid., 59.

39 *JI*, XXXIII (January 15, 1898), 69-70.

40 Ibid.

41 *JI*, XXXIV (February 15, 1899), 110-11.

by Church members for transportation.[42]

The Spanish custom of bullfighting was attacked in a brief article in the *Juvenile Instructor*. Bullfighting was blamed for creating a "love for bloodshed" and a "desire to see pain."[43] Latter-day Saints were expected by the magazine to desire "harmony between animals and man" and not "bloodshed."[44]

The Cannon publication cited an interesting study on crime that supported a zoophilic quality in man. The study revealed that teachings about kindness to animals or the ownership of pets was a definite deterrent to crime.[45]

At the age of seventy-two and after having served as a counselor to three Presidents of The Church of Jesus Christ of Latter-day Saints, George Q. Cannon was still writing about the humane treatment of animals. One of his last editorials began with an expressed doubt as to the success or usefulness of bounties on predators. He specifically attacked the hunting of hawks. Reporting that one state had paid "nearly a hundred thousand dollars" to destroy hawks, President Cannon quoted an authority as saying each hawk was worth twenty dollars even after deducting the cost of chickens it had killed. The value of the hawk was determined by the number of mice and other rodents it normally consumed. The crow and the coyote were likewise defended by editor Cannon. Basically his argument in the editorial was that "efforts to destroy the equilibrium [of nature] are generally disastrous."[46] He closed the editorial with the comments:

---

42 Ibid., 113-14.

43 *JI*, XXXIII (May, 1989), 565-66.

44 Ibid.

45 *JI*, XXV (February, 1900), 124.

46 *JI*, XXXIV (April, 1899), 492-93.

> To inflict pain or death unnecessarily upon any of the creations of our Father is not a commendable pursuit. To delight in slaughter and blood is not an indication of a pure, good heart. Besides, how is the time to come when enmity between man and beast shall cease, when a little child shall be safe in playing with and leading the most savage animal—how is the world to reach an era of universal peace, if man, the superior animal, does not himself take the first steps toward it by getting rid of his blood-thirstiness and by regarding all life as sacred.[47]

The February, 1901 *Juvenile Instructor* printed a "reminder" about the annual Humane Day services. Though the Deseret Sunday School Union had purchased the *Juvenile Instructor* in 1900, George Q. Cannon remained as editor of the publication and superintendent of the Sunday School until his death, April 17, 1901. The "reminder" bears evidence of at least President Cannon's influence if not his pen when it requested that addresses be delivered in the Sunday School services which would "set forth in as forcible manner as possible the propriety of being kind and considerate to the animal kingdom" and would teach children to show "kindness, consideration, mercy, forbearance, and love toward all the living creations of God."[48]

President George Q. Cannon's lifelong endeavor to promote kindness to the animal world was to be continued by his successor to the editorship of the *Juvenile Instructor*, President Joseph F. Smith.

---

47 Ibid., 493.

48 *JI*, XXXVI (February, 1901), 84.

Chapter 5

President Joseph F. Smith and Kindness to Animals

During the twentieth century all of the Presidents of The Church of Jesus Christ of Latter-day Saints have made statements relating to zoophily.

Lorenzo Snow, President of the Church from September, 1898, to October, 1901, recorded an incident about hunting at the age of twenty-four when living in Missouri. Said President Snow: "While moving slowly forward in pursuit of something to kill, my mind was arrested with the reflection on the nature of my pursuit—that of amusing myself by giving pain and death to harmless, innocent creatures that perhaps had as much right to life and enjoyment as myself. I realized that such indulgence was without any justification, and feeling condemned, I laid my gun on my shoulder, returned home, and from that time to this have felt no inclination for that murderous amusement."[1] The experience was evidently deeply impressed upon his mind as it is noted in 1897 that he thought the Word of Wisdom was

> ...violated as much or more in the improper use of meat as in other things, and thought the time was near at hand when the Latter-day Saints should be taught to refrain from meat eating and the shedding of animal blood. [2]

---

1 Thomas C. Romney, *The Life of Lorenzo Snow* (Salt Lake City: SUP Memorial Foundation, 1955), 35.

2 Journal History, November 3, 1897, as cited in Leonard J. Arrington, "An Economic Interpretation of the Word of Wisdom," *BYU Studies*, I, (Winter,

Joseph F. Smith, successor to Lorenzo Snow as President of the Church in 1901, had an experience similar to President Snow's that left him with no desire to hurt animals. As President Smith related the incident to the membership of the Church in general conference, he recalled the time of his baptism when a feeling of pure peace and love came over him. He added that he "felt as though I wanted to do good everywhere to everybody and to everything." In fact, he stated that he felt he "would not injure the smallest insect" beneath his feet.[3]

Joseph F. Smith became President of the Church, superintendent of the Sunday Schools of the Church, and editor of the *Juvenile Instructor* on October 17, 1901. He retained all three positions until his death, November 18, 1918. It was in his role as editor of the then official Sunday School magazine, the *Juvenile Instructor*, that President Smith most frequently spoke on the subject of kindness to animals.

There were frequent editorials pertaining to zoophily in the *Juvenile Instructor*, as there had been previously under the editorship of George Q. Cannon. The content of these editorial remarks reflected President Smith's great concern for animal life. From 1902 to 1907 the magazine carried on its first page a series of articles to be used by the Sunday School on Humane Day. These articles appeared in the February issue annually. Because of President Smith's trio of duties it was evident that the emphasis on Humane Day and the publication of articles supporting it were the desire of President Smith, the man accepted as the spokesman for God on earth by members of the Church. The first series was the lengthiest, running sixteen pages. The articles were generally of a story nature with moralizing comments interspersed. Titles in the first series were indicative of the content. Titles in the initial issue included "The Robin in the Church," "A Faithful Animal," and "President Lincoln's Kindness." Stories which emphasized certain qualities in the animal world included "A Spider's Genius," "Cautious Ducks," and "A Dog's

---

1959), 47.

3 Conference Report (Salt Lake City: The Church of Jesus Christ of Latter-day Saints,1898), 66. Hereafter cited as CR.

Jealousy." Other articles intended to promote sympathy for animals and examples included "Birds Recognize a Benefactor," "A Parrot's Fire Alarm," "The Horses Wounded in Battle," and "How Birds Dress Wounds."[4]

The following year, 1903, the space devoted to humane articles was limited to thirteen pages and by 1907 it was only seven pages. Even though the number of pages was limited, zoophily was represented by twelve articles.[5] Various later issues of the *Juvenile Instructor* printed articles on animals though the formal series was discontinued.

Formal editorial content concerning kindness to animals was at first limited to the Humane Day program and were unsigned. An early example was the lengthy front page editorial of the February, 1907, publication. The editorial was very reminiscent of George Q. Cannon's writing. The editorial praised the thought that prompted Humane Day observance in the Sunday Schools. The responsibility to punish animals was discussed. It was suggested by the anonymous writer that punishment of animals should be done with consideration of their "intelligence and the real necessities of the case."[6] Considered more important than the cruelty done to animals was the effect the cruelty had upon the human being administering the cruelty. The explanation was that "doing wrong to animals" was a "stepping stone to the doing of wrong to our fellow men."[7] An example was given of a boy who was cruel to a team of mules. The boy lost his temper because of the stubborn mules and "in time there was a spirit of noticeable cruelty towards his companions." The writer commented that he had "seen boys unfortunately associated with vicious [sic] teams." The writer proposed a concept new to *Juvenile Instructor* editorials concerning animals when

---

4 *JI*, XXXVII (February, 1902), 97-112.

5 *JI*, XLII (February, 1907), 97-103.

6 Ibid., 97.

7 Ibid.

he stated that "all teams are not good and desirable, anymore than all men are so."[8] Referring to the female readers, the writer said they were naturally more tender than boys but that they also were often cruel. The reason for cruelty by women was given to be a "lack of sympathy" and that women often considered an animal as a "mere machine."[9]

A short announcement of Humane Day in 1911 commented favorably on recent legislation to protect animals in the United States. However, the "editorial thought" was that while the passage of laws was helpful, education was the more effective approach to avoid cruelty to animals. It was stated that kindness to animals should be "a matter of principle, not law."[10] The editor suggested that children "be taught from infancy to be kind and tender" to the animals under human care. Further, he stated: "When every soul gets into the condition of mind that he will go out of his way to ease the suffering of a dumb animal, then many of the cruelties now complained of will disappear from the earth forever."[11]

The editors concluded with the pronouncement that they would "join with all good citizens in the effort to awaken the public conscience in regard to this subject" of kindness to animals.[12]

The first editorial article on animals directly attributed to President Joseph F. Smith was in February, 1912. President Smith began by quoting from Proverbs concerning the "righteous man regardeth the life of his beast; but the tender mercies of the wicked are cruel." He reflected that man "to a very large extent" had been selfish, thoughtless, and cruel. He recounted an incident wherein a farm hand had left a porcupine suffering in the throes of death and contrasted the concern of

---

8 Ibid., 98.

9 Ibid.

10 *JI*, XLVI (February, 1911), 83.

11 Ibid.

12 Ibid.

a humane individual for it. President Smith wrote that kindness to all animals was "the absolute duty of mankind." He further stated that the man who mistreats an animal "disqualifies himself for the companionship of the Holy Spirit."[13]

The love of animals was the headlined topic of an editorial thought by Joseph F. Smith in 1913. He opened with a word of commendation for the annual Humane Day program of the Church, saying it had brought happiness to people and "great good to the animals themselves."[14] President Smith wrote that kindness brought joy to men and comfort to animals "even when practiced towards the lowest of creatures."[15] Man's happiness is increased because of his kindness to animals for two reasons, wrote President Smith. Freedom from fear of man made for better relations between man and beast. Also beneficial to man was "improved conditions of thought and feeling" in man.

Specific examples of benefits derived from man's exercise of kindness to animals were cited by President Smith in his editorial. The first example was of dairy cattle in Holland and Denmark which were reportedly "not even harshly spoken to." As a result, stated President Smith, the dairyman because of his gentleness, was "both better and richer" as an individual.[16] A second example was the treatment of horses in La Perdie, France. President Smith proposed that the Percheron horse was both kinder and more intelligent than other animals as a result of the kind treatment of its trainers. Asking why kindness contributed to intelligence, President Smith answered his own question by saying it was because "kindness is an attribute of intelligence."

Animals also possess the attribute of love, President Smith wrote. President Smith held that "all nature responds to love," and the result is

---

13 *JI*, XLVII (February, 1912), 78-79. See Appendix for the complete text.

14 Joseph F. Smith, "The Love of Animals," *JI*, XLVIII (February, 1913), 84.

15 Ibid.

16 Ibid.

contentment for man and nature. Concluding his editorial President Smith declared that it was "both duty and wisdom" to show "loving kindness" to animals.[17]

Two months after the above editorial appeared, President Joseph F. Smith spoke to the Deseret Sunday School Union in his dual capacity as President of the Church and superintendent of its Sunday Schools. The remarks were reprinted in the next issue of the *Juvenile Instructor* as "editorial thoughts."[18] President Smith remarked favorably on previous speakers who had spoken in a zoophilic fashion. He then specifically referred to the "killing of our innocent little birds." He stated his opinion that "it is not only wicked to destroy them it is abominable."

He elucidated on his personal feelings when he said that he "never could see why a man should be imbued with a bloodthirsty desire to kill" animal life. He stated as his belief that man should not "kill animals or birds unless he needs them for food." The further qualification was made that man should "not kill innocent little birds that are not intended as food for man." He reiterated his earlier comment that he thought it was "wicked for men to thirst in their souls to kill almost everything which possesses animal life."[19] He concluded his remarks by stating:

> It is wrong, and I have been surprised at prominent men whom I have seen whose very souls seemed to be athirst for the shedding of animal blood. They go off hunting deer, antelope, elk, anything they can find, and what for? "Just for the fun of it!" Not that they are hungry and need the flesh of their prey, but just because they love to shoot and to destroy life. I am a firm believer, with reference to these things, in the simple words of one of the poets: "Take not away

---

17 Ibid., 85.

18 Joseph F. Smith, "The Destruction of Animal Life," *JI*, XLVIII (May, 1913), 308-9.

19 Ibid.

the life you cannot give, For all things have an equal right to life."[20]

The ecological concern of the balance of nature was emphasized in an unsigned editorial of the *Juvenile Instructor*, June, 1915. The opening paragraph recalled that "young people have long been admonished to protect the birds, that they in turn may protect us."[21] Reference was made to bounties paid to exterminate hawks and owls in Pennsylvania, which was later regretted with the increase in rodents.

The editorial stated that "God in His wisdom has established a wonderful economic balance in the distribution of His creations" and man suffers whenever the balance is disturbed.[22] Admitting that birds may eat fruit and grain, the writer held that "the laborer is worthy of his hire." Birds labored for the grower earlier in the spring by devouring insects, the writer commented, and if they ate some fruit for their sustenance, "they are surely entitled to it."[23] The ecological concern of the writer was summarized by his statement:

> If we could understand all the purposes of God in His Wonderful creations, we could avoid diligently the dangers of disturbing the balance in the distribution of life which God has so wonderfully ordained.[24]

Birds received special attention by the Sunday School superintendency consisting of President Joseph F. Smith, David O. McKay, and Stephen L. Richards, in 1915. They announced in the *Juvenile Instructor*, that a special "Bird Day" was to be celebrated in all

---

20 Ibid., 309.

21 *JI*, L (June, 1915), 372.

22 Ibid.

23 Ibid., 373.

24 Ibid.

Sunday Schools of the Church with talks aimed at protecting bird life. The announcement stated that "kindness to animals and all living things" was a "good way of expressing true religion."[25] Cruelty to animals, continued the brief article, "always shows an absence of the true religious spirit" and was considered "barbarous."[26]

Also during Joseph F. Smith's time as Church President, superintendent of the Sunday Schools, and editor of the *Juvenile Instructor*, a special editorial on "Humane Day" was published. Signatures accompanying the editorial were of the Sunday School superintendency, which included the future President of the Church, David O. McKay, and Stephen L. Richards, later counselor in the First Presidency to David O. McKay.

This same editorial was repeated by Heber J. Grant, successor to Joseph F. Smith as President of The Church of Jesus Christ of Latter-day Saints and editor of the *Juvenile Instructor*. Thus three Presidents of the Church gave their endorsement and published this important statement on zoophily in the Church. Because of its unique status this document is also reproduced in full.

> What is it to be humane to the beasts of the fields and the birds of the air? It is more than to be considerate of the animal life entrusted to our care. It is a grateful appreciation of God's creations. It is the lesson of divine law. To Him all life is a sacred creation for the use of His children. Do we stand beside Him in our tender regard for life?
>
> Our sense of appreciation should be quickened by a desire to understand divine purposes, and to keep the balance of animal life adjusted to the needs of creation. Man in his wanton disregard of a sacred duty has been reckless of life. He has destroyed it with an indifference to the evil results it would entail upon the earth. Birds have been uselessly slaughtered, and pests have sprung up as a consequence to plague the people of the world. We are a part of all

---

25 *JI*, L (June, 1915), 375.

26 Ibid.

> life and should study carefully our relationship to it. We should be in sympathy with it, and not allow our prejudices to create a desire for its destruction. The unnecessary destruction of life begets a spirit of destruction which grows within the soul. It lives by what it feeds upon and robs man of the love that he should have for the works of God. It hardens the heart of man and makes him prey upon the social welfare which he should feel for the happiness and advancement of his fellow man.
>
> The unnecessary destruction of life is a distinct spiritual loss to the human family. Men cannot worship the Creator and look with careless indifference upon his creation. The love of all life helps man to the enjoyment of a better life. It exalts the spiritual nature of those in need of divine favor. The wanton destruction of life reacts upon the human family. There is something of the law of compensation which makes criminals injure and destroy life. Men who are unsympathetic toward the life of domestic animals entrusted to them usually receive the reward of the cruelty by the dumb animals which they maltreat. Love begets love in all creation, and nature responds bounteously to the tender treatment of man.
>
> Men learn more easily in sympathetic relationships of all life than they do in the seclusion of human interest. Their minds are more open to the manifestations of that inspiration which all nature gives to those who lovingly enjoy her. Wisdom and virtue come from the animal and vegetable world which carries with it a spiritual as well as a material blessing. Nature helps us to see and understand God. To all His creations we owe an allegiance of service and a profound admiration. Man should be kind to the animals which serve him both directly and indirectly. An angry word or a brutal blow wounds the heart from which is comes. Love of nature is akin to the love of God; the two are inseparable.[27]

The most official statement of the Church, outside of the accepted books of scripture, concerning animals was a statement during the administration of Joseph F. Smith over the signatures of the First Presidency. The Presidency in the official declaration stated that God

---

27 *JI*, LIII (April, 1918), 182-83; *JI*, LXII (April, 1927), 190-91.

"made the tadpole and the ape, the lion and the elephant; but He did not make them in His own image, nor endow them with Godlike reason and intelligence. Nevertheless, the whole animal creation will be perfected and perpetuated in the Hereafter, each class in its 'distinct order or sphere,' and will enjoy 'eternal felicity.' That fact has been made plain in this dispensation (Doctrine and Covenants 77:3)."[28]

In retrospect it may be noted that President Joseph F. Smith became the most ardent advocate of any President of The Church of Jesus Christ of Latter-day Saints for the cause of zoophily in published articles. During his tenure as President the annual Humane Day and Bird Day were given strong support by his writing.

---

28 "The Origin of Man," *Improvement Era*, XIII (November, 1909), 81.

Chapter 6

David O. Mckay and Joseph Fielding Smith: Advocates for Animals

Following the death of President Joseph F. Smith, Heber J. Grant became the seventh President of The Church of Jesus Christ of Latter-day Saints. President Grant left no published record of zoophilic principles except endorsing the previously quoted editorial written by Joseph F. Smith and his two counselors in the Sunday School organization of the Church. He did, however, make reference to his near vegetarian habits in a general conference of the Church held in the famed tabernacle in Salt Lake City. At the age of eighty he declared:

> I think that another reason I have very splendid strength for an old man is that during the years we have had a cafeteria in the Utah Hotel I have not, with the exception of not more than a dozen times, ordered meat of any kind. One of these special occasions I have mentioned I have perhaps had a small tender lamb chop. I have endeavored to live the Word of Wisdom, and that, in my opinion, is one reason for my good health.[1]

President Grant remained active until his death, May 15, 1945 at the age of eighty-eight.

George Albert Smith succeeded Heber J. Grant as President of the Church. Living to the age of eighty-one, President Smith was, like Heber J. Grant, a practitioner of the sparing use of meat in his diet. His son-in-law recorded during President Smith's lifetime, "In the summer

---

1 Conference Report (Salt Lake City: The Church of Jesus Christ of Latter-day Saints, April, 1937), 15.

he eats no meat, and even in the winter months he eats very little."[2]

President Smith was succeeded as President of the Church by David O. McKay in 1951. As counselor to Joseph F. Smith in the Sunday School superintendency of the Church, President McKay had close association with the staunch advocate of kindness to animals. During that period President McKay wrote a lengthy article for the "Superintendent's Department" of the *Juvenile Instructor*, which served as the official publication for the Sunday School. Decrying the use of bird feathers for women's millinery, he wrote that "greed and vanity combine to destroy...some of the most beautiful of God's creatures."[3] Referring to the "murder" of birds, he said the fate of the egret was "tragic." Appealing to the sensitiveness of his readers, President McKay portrayed "the suffering of these helpless fledglings slowly dying, and calling in vain for the mother that never returns." He then proposed that it was time that "every organization in the world" should act to protect birds. "True religion [is] imparted" by exercising "love for all the creatures of the earth," emphasized President McKay.[4]

After becoming President of the Church, David O. McKay spoke of kindness to animals in two of the general conferences of the Church. In 1951 he commented that "a true Latter-day Saint is kind to animals, is kind to every created thing, for God has created all."[5] President McKay mentioned scenes of cruelty he had witnessed during a trip to the Near East. "However," reminded President McKay, one need not go to the Near East to see cruelty, for it is "around here if we but open our eyes." He then suggested that it was "a good thing to teach our boys to be

---

2 Robert Murray Stewart, "A Normal Day in the Home of George Albert Smith," *The Improvement Era*, LIII (April, 1950), 287.

3 David O. McKay, "Protect the Birds," *JI* XLVIII (May, 1913), 310.

4 Ibid., 311.

5 CR, October, 1951, 180.

kind."[6] President McKay related an incident that occurred on his farm. An employee reported to him at the close of the day that he had killed a porcupine. When the President asked why he had done so, the man replied, "Oh, just for fun." Asked if the animal was still suffering, the worker assured him he had killed it.President McKay, however, still concerned, reported going to the site of the cruelty and found the porcupine still struggling for life. He concluded the account with the statement, "What fun can there be in treating dumb animals in that cruel way!"[7]

In the opening address of conference held in April, 1952, President McKay summarized the activities of the various auxiliary organizations of the Church. Referring to the Primary organization for children under the age of twelve, President McKay made special mention of the "Kindness to Animals Club" sponsored by the Primary in their publication, the *Children's Friend.* He commended it to the attention of the audience and said it was a "very commendable feature."[8]

A biographer of David O. McKay began a chapter entitled "Kindness to Animals" with the sentence: "One of the characteristics which has marked the life of President David O. McKay is his love of animals."[9] Throughout the chapter, examples are given of the youthful David exhibiting kind concern for pets. Included were such creatures as a dog, pigeons, rabbits, a wounded magpie, and the many horses with names such as Kate, Puss, Prince, Charlie, and Sonny Boy, which elicited the comment that "President McKay's love for horses is

---

6 Ibid.

7 Ibid.

8 CR, April, 1952, 13.

9 Jeanette McKay Morell, *Highlights in the Life of President David O. McKay* (Salt Lake City: Deseret Book Co., 1966), 288.

proverbial."[10] In commenting on the treatment of horses, the President once remarked about a trainer: "He uses the whip too freely and I don't want my horses mistreated." President McKay further stated that "they can be trained with kindness much more effectively."[11]

Two incidents are recorded to show President McKay's concern for all animals. The first concerns a bird. President McKay had left a window open in a locked saddle house. Because of a previous theft the house was locked, but he had left the window open to allow a bird to fly into its nest on the inside. When his sisters informed him of the danger of leaving an open window, adding that they had shut it, he became concerned and insisted on driving back to the farm to reopen it. He commented on his return to the sisters that a "little bird was outside trying to get in, and the mother was inside attempting to get out."[12]

The second incident is very likely the same incident referred to in Joseph F. Smith's editorial on "Kindness to Animals" previously quoted, the incident of the porcupine being mercifully cared for.[13] One of the general authorities of the Church serving under President McKay identifies him as performing the service of mercy. Using the "ideal teacher" as his model, Boyd K. Packer related a descriptive story: "Once or twice when I worked with him outside the classroom, I recognized a reverence for life, something you see, for instance, in Albert Schweitzer. David O. McKay was once informed by his farmhand that he had killed a porcupine over the edge of the grove. 'But did you kill it?' asked President McKay. 'Oh, yes,' replied the farmhand, 'I dispatched it with a stick.' And David O. McKay, apostle, climbed over the fence, walked across the field, and found the animal critically and painfully injured but not killed. He mercifully killed it. That interest, that compassion, that

---

10 Ibid., 292.

11 Ibid., 294.

12 Ibid., 295.

13 Supra, 91, 101.

reverence for life, is characteristic of the teacher I describe."[14]

President McKay is thus added to the list of those holding positions of leadership in The Church of Jesus Christ of Latter-day Saints who espoused kindness to animals. That others of the Church leadership were influenced by him is evidenced by the above citation of Boyd K. Packer, who became an apostle in April, 1970.

The tenth President of The Church of Jesus Christ of Latter-day Saints, Joseph Fielding Smith, continued his father, Joseph F. Smith's, concern for animal welfare. While yet a young apostle, President Joseph Fielding Smith stated in a general conference of the Church:

> So we see that the Lord intends to save, not only the earth and the heavens, not only man who dwells upon the earth, but all things which he has created. The animals, the fishes of the sea, the fowls of the air, as well as man, are to be resurrected, or renewed, through the resurrection, for they too are living souls.[15]

On another occasion Joseph Fielding Smith qualified the status of animals by stating that the gift of conscience "was not given to the animal world!"[16] He further commented that "the Lord does not require of them repentance from sin, for they do not sin. It requires intelligence and a knowledge of right and wrong, in order for a man to sin. While animals prey on each other there is no violation of conscience, for they have not the gift of conscience. There is no moral obligation for a lion or a bear, or any other carnivorous animal to kill and prey on other animals, for the Lord did not give to them the light of truth.... There is no moral question troubling them. They have no moral sense, of

---

14 Boyd K. Packer, "The Ideal Teacher," Provo, Utah: Seminaries and Institutes, June 28, 1962, 5. (Mimeographed.)

15 CR, October, 1928, 99-100.

16 Joseph Fielding Smith, *Man: His Origin and Destiny* (Salt Lake City: Deseret Book Co., 1954), 204; emphasis in original.

understanding of justice, right or wrong."[17]

In the *Improvement Era*, an official publication of the Church, President Smith clarified a point of doctrine concerning the status of animals as immortal beings after the resurrection.

"The simple answer is that animals do have spirits and that through the redemption made by our Savior they will come forth in the resurrection to enjoy the blessing of immortal life."[18] As to the location and character of their existence after the resurrection President Smith further stated:

> As to where the beasts, birds, and fish, and all other creatures will go after the resurrection we can only express an opinion. John saw many of them in heaven in the presence of God. It is very probable that they, like mankind, will be distributed in the various kingdoms, celestial, terrestrial and telestial. We may well believe that in each of these kingdoms such creatures will be assigned.[19]

Referring to the millennial condition of animals and man, President Smith has said: " What did Isaiah say? Before you get through asking I will answer. The lion, as well as the lamb, these animals that are now so filled with vicious habits will then be at peace, and so it says here there will be no enmity between man and beast, and we will not delight to go off and kill deer when that time comes.[20]

In a course of study for the Church, Joseph Fielding Smith criticized the hunting of animals for sport. Said he:

---

17 Ibid., 205.

18 Joseph Fielding Smith, "Your Question," *The Improvement Era*, LXI (January, 1958), 16-17.

19 Ibid., 17.

20 Joseph Fielding Smith, *Signs of the Times* (Salt Lake City: Deseret Book Co., 1964), 36.

> It is a grievous sin in the sight of God to kill merely for sport. Such a thing shows a weakness in the spiritual character of the individual. We cannot restore life when it is taken, and all creatures have the right to enjoy life and happiness on the earth where the Lord has placed them. Only for food, and then sparingly, should flesh be eaten, for all life is from God and is eternal.[21]

Discussing the Word of Wisdom and its advice to eat meat sparingly, the tenth prophet of The Church of Jesus Christ of Latter-day Saints has said:

> Neither is it the intent of this revelation to include grains and fruits in the restrictions placed upon meats, that they should be used only in famine or excess of hunger. The antecedent of "these" in verse fifteen may not be clear, but common sense teaches us that it does not refer to grain in the preceding verse. While it is ordained that the flesh of animals is for man's food, (Section 48:18-19 [in the Doctrine and Covenants]) yet this should be used sparingly. The wording of this revelation is perfectly clear in relation to this subject, but we do not always heed it.[22]

In personal practice, President Smith is reported to have a "disdain of meat and love of vegetables."[23] His late wife Jessie Evans revealed that "my husband doesn't eat meat," but rather "lots of fruit and vegetables."[24]

It was during President Smith's term that a reorganization of the

---

21 Joseph Fielding Smith, *Church History and Modern Revelation* (n.p.: Council of the Twelve Apostles of The Church of Jesus Christ of Latter-day Saints, 1947), I, 210.

22 Ibid., II, 148.

23 *BYU Daily Universe*, XXIII (May 6, 1971), 1.

24 *The Improvement Era*, LXXIII (April, 1970), 59.

Church magazines occurred. The last comment on animals in the *Improvement Era* was an article about newly selected apostle Boyd K. Packer. It remarked on his great love of nature and especially birds.[25] *The Instructor*, the magazine for Church teachers, ran its final article relating to animals in the August, 1970, issue.[26] It concerned anointing for healing of pioneer oxen.

The new magazines for English-speaking Saints were the *Friend*, for children, the *New Era*, for those approximately twelve to twenty-five, and the *Ensign*, for adults.

The *Friend* has featured stories involving animals in virtually every issue. Perhaps the most explicit attempt to instill humaneness was the "advertisement" taken from the American Humane Association for "Be Kind to Animals Day" in the May, 1977, issue.

The *New Era* of 1972 had a number of articles relating to animals. The January issue mentioned the love of Joseph F. Smith for his oxen.[27] The May issue had an article on the Gospel and ecology.[28] Dr. Hugh Nibley had a very important article in the October issue on "Man's Dominion." Dr. Nibley pointed out that there have been two traditions of dominion: unrighteous and exploitive, symbolized by Nimrod the hunter, and the contrasting view of dominion as stewardship, represented by Abraham and the prophets.[29]

The year 1972 saw my article on the "Gospel and Animals" in

---

25 Jay Todd, "Boyd K. Packer," *IE* (May 1970), 4-8.

26 Marie Felt, "With Oxcart and Courage to Salt Lake Valley," *The Instructor* (Aug. 1970), 294.

27 "Joseph F Smith: Families and Generation Gaps," *The New Era* (Jan. 1972), 40.

28 Robert Matthews, "What the Scriptures Say About Ecology," *The New Era* (May, 1972), 38-39.

29 Hugh Nibley, "Man's Dominion," *The New Era* (October, 1972).

August.[30] This was followed in March, 1977, by answers to questions concerning animals.[31] In 1978 we saw an emphasis in general conference by President Spencer W. Kimball on being kind to animals and birds. He referred to a song he had learned as a child about not killing birds.[32] In the October priesthood session of general conference President Kimball strongly denounced killing for sport and quoted Joseph Smith and Joseph F. Smith extensively on the topic. He declared the destruction of wildlife "wicked." These talks were printed in the *Ensign* and given attention in the *Church News*.[33]

Though not equaling in quantity the amount of zoophilic material published by President Joseph F. Smith, his successors as Presidents of The Church of Jesus Christ of Latter-day Saints have all indicated they were in harmony with his teachings. No written record has indicated any opposition in any way, and indeed, Presidents David O. McKay, Joseph Fielding Smith, and Spencer W. Kimball have repeated his concerns for animal life.

---

30 Gerald E. Jones, "The Gospel and Animals," *The Ensign* (August 1972), 62-65.

31 _______""Where Do Animals Fit in the Eternal Plan of Things," *The Ensign* (March, 1977), 61-62.

32 Spencer W. Kimball, "Strengthening the Family," *The Ensign* (April, 1977), 46-53

33 _________ "Fundamental Principles to Ponder and Live," *The Ensign* (Nov. 1978), 44-45.

Chapter 7

Official Humane Programs of the Latter-day Saints

The earliest known official humane program sponsored by The Church of Jesus Christ of Latter-day Saints was an annual Humane Day. The commemoration of Humane Day was held in the Sunday Schools of the Church during the month of February. The program was publicly announced in the *Juvenile Instructor*, January 15, 1897, by George Q. Cannon. Elder Cannon was serving as first counselor in the First Presidency of the Church under President Wilford Woodruff and as Superintendent of the Sunday School organization. The *Juvenile Instructor* was the official publication of the Sunday Schools of the Church, though published by President Cannon. The announcement read:

> The Deseret Sunday School Union Board have discussed the propriety of doing something in the direction of impressing the children with lessons concerning the proper treatment of animals, and have appointed Sunday, February 28th, as HUMANE DAY. In appointing this as Humane Day it is the design to have the usual services and lessons taken upon that day in the Sunday School, in their regular order; but that in addition to these, addresses be given by persons selected for this purpose, which will set forth in as forcible a manner as possible the propriety of being kind and considerate to the animal creation, especially those domestic animals with which children are most closely brought in contact. The object of these addresses will be to teach the children kindness, mercy,

forbearance and love toward all the living creations of God.[1]

President Cannon proceeded at some length in the same article to stress the principle of kindness to animals.

Further information on the origin of Humane Day was given by Karl G. Maeser at a conference of the Deseret Sunday School Union in April, 1899. Superintendent Maeser indicated that a letter from an unidentified woman in the Church to the Sunday School may have sparked the beginning of the annual day for kindness to animals.[2]

The Humane Day commemoration was changed from February to April in 1916 in a directive of the general superintendency of the Sunday School, which then consisted of Joseph F. Smith (also President of the Church at the time), David O. McKay, and Stephen L. Richards. The change was to conform to the National Humane Society emphasis for Humane Day on the last Sunday of April.[3] The last emphasis placed on the Humane Day program was by the general superintendency in an editorial of April, 1918.[4] This editorial was later repeated verbatim in the April, 1927, issue of the *Juvenile Instructor*, but no further emphasis has been discovered in the Sunday School organization of the Church since 1918.[5]

As found in the preceding chapters on George Q. Cannon and Joseph F. Smith, there were numerous editorials in the *Juvenile Instructor* every month the special day was celebrated. From five to sixteen pages of zoophilic material were produced to serve as

---

1 George Q. Cannon, "Topics for the Times," *The Juvenile Instructor*, XXIX (January, 1897), 59.

2 CR, April, 1899, 76-77.

3 *JI*, LII (April, 1916), 193.

4 *JI*, LIII (April, 1918), 182-83.

5 *JI*, LXII (April, 1927), 190-91.

supplementary information for local Sunday School officers and teachers, as well as for general readership from 1902 to 1918. Some of the articles were reprinted from national humane publications and others were editorially produced.[6]

There was also a short-lived program on kindness to birds during the same period as the Humane Day episode. In 1912 the first Sunday of August was designated to bring a "better appreciation and protection of the birds."[7] The following year assistant superintendent David O. McKay, later President of The Church of Jesus Christ of Latter-day Saints, wrote a lengthy article asking for increased protection for birds. President McKay's article also announced that June 1 was designated as Bird Day.[8] The first Sunday of June, 1915, appears to be the last commemoration of Bird Day in the Sunday School organization as no further reference is given to the celebration of the day in published works.

Though the Sunday School has not sponsored any official programs since 1918, the year Joseph F. Smith died, there have been articles concerning zoophily in the *Instructor* magazine with titles such as, "Do You Treat Your Pets with Kindness?"[9] "Reverence for Life,"[10] and "Thou Shalt Not Kill."[11] Intended as a supplement to a Sunday School lesson on the sixth commandment, "Do You Treat Your Pet with Kindness?" stressed the need for animals to be "loved and treated with

---

6 *JI*, XXVII (February, 1902), 97-112; *JI*, LII (April, 1917), 171-76. Supra, 88-97.

7 "Bird Day in Sunday Schools," *JI*, XLVII (February 1912), 78-79.

8 *JI*, XLVIII (May, 1913), 310-11.

9 James G. Lawrence, *Instructor*, IIIC (May, 1962), 154-55.

10 Lowell L. Bennion, *Instructor*, XC (May, 1960), 164-65.

11 Lowell L. Jackson, *Instructor*, IVC (May, 1964), 179-81.

kindness at all times."[12] The author related activities of three leaders in the Humane movement—Albert Schweitzer, Andrew Hallide, and Henry Bergh. The article was introduced by a phrase from a popular commentary on a Church scripture: "Man has been entrusted with sovereignty over the animal kingdom, that he may learn to govern, as God rules, by the power of love and justice."[13]

"Reverence for Life" was an article published to be used by teachers of three different courses of the Sunday School in 1960. The name of Albert Schweitzer is prominent in the article, first by a sketch of his activity in a hospital. The caption of the sketch of Schweitzer stressed his concept of "reverence for life." The editor's preface to the article stated that "an attitude of respect or reverence for life is one thing that will help a person to exercise self-control in human relations."[14] The article reminds the youth that God "does not want man to hurt and kill animals and people needlessly," He would rather have youth "show respect for life as [did] Albert Schweitzer."[15]

The article on killing contained a prefatory "note to the teacher" which stated that "this article is written to discourage wanton killing. The teacher should discriminate between hunting for food and killing for fun."[16] The body of the article told of some grey geese flying south for the winter. When one of them was shot down the hunter asked himself the question whether "this senseless killing for mere pleasure was right."[17]

---

12 Lawrence, 154-55.

13 Ibid., 154.

14 Bennion, 164.

15 Ibid., 165.

16 Jackson, 179.

17 Ibid., 181.

The Primary organization, for children under the age of twelve, began to stress humane treatment of animals in 1902 with the first issue of their official magazine, the *Children's Friend.*[18] In a lesson on kindness the story was told of a horse that was beaten even though it was doing its best to carry a load. When kindness was shown to the horse it responded with the desired efforts. The lesson learned was that "love is the best force."[19]

The following year a lesson on mercy was presented. The central story of the lesson concerned a wounded and lost dog that responded to kind care.[20]

A lesson for the Primary given in 1907 related the Joseph Smith incident with rattlesnakes on the Zion Camp expedition. References were made in the article about Henry Bergh, Abraham Lincoln, and others who were examples of kindness to animals. The article stated that "every boy and girl can help in the good work of helping animals and make the world better and happier by being kind to them and persuading other boys and girls to be fair to them."[21]

Another lesson on kindness was presented to the Primary children through the pages of the *Children's Friend* in 1910. The lesson referred to Rebekah giving food and water to camels in the Bible story of Isaac and Rebekah. It also referred to David caring for sheep and suggested it was "right to be kind to all animals."[22]

A special lesson on animals was given in a 1911 *Children's Friend.* An opening sentence proclaimed that "kindness to animals, especially to beasts of burden, is an index to a noble character." Examples given

---

18 *The Children's Friend*, I, (January, 1902), 12-13. Hereafter *CF.*

19 *CF*, I, (October, 1902), 318-19.

20 *CF*, II (May, 1903), 180-82.

21 *CF*, VI (January, 1907), 23-29.

22 *CF*, IX (May, 1910), 266-67.

included stories about Daniel Webster being kind to his oxen and Benedict Arnold being cruel to birds and animals.[23] Abraham Lincoln's stopping to pick up a bird and replacing it in its nest was retold in a lesson on "Elijah and the Widow."[24] It was suggested that Lincoln performed such acts "because his brave heart was full of gentleness and love for all the things his Heavenly Father made and loved."[25]

The "cruel pleasure of killing" was the subject of a story about a group of picnickers excitedly trying to kill a large snake, which was related in a 1911 issue of the *Children's Friend.*[26]

Except for scattered articles, there was no renewed emphasis in the *Children's Friend* until the 1940s. In 1941 a special section was placed in the magazine entitled "Pets."[27] In 1946 and 1947 there were special lessons in zoophily for members in the missions of the Church.[28] In September, 1950, it was announced that the Pet Page would become the "Kindness to Animals Page" beginning January, 1951.[29] From December of 1957 until 1971 there was no special page devoted to animals. The magazine appealed to young children, and the emphasis on animals was often strengthened with pictures, short poems, and games concerning animals. For example, in 1966 there were approximately 125 pages concerning animals in the *Children's Friend*, but there was no

---

23 *CF*, X (January, 1911), 47.

24 *CF*, X (May, 1911), 257.

25 Ibid.

26 *CF*, X (December, 1911), 665.

27 *CF*, XL (January, 1941), 30, 82, 128.

28 *CF*, XLV (June, 1946), 268-69; *CF*, XLVI (April, 1947), 177-79, and (November, 1947), 501-502.

29 *CF*, XLIX (September, 1950), 383.

stress on kindness to animals.[30]

An important program sponsored by the Primary organization in the *Children's Friend* was called the "Kindness to Animals Club," referred to frequently in the publication as "KTA." The announcement inviting Primary children to join the club was in the January, 1952 issue.[31] On the top half of the page was a banner headline inviting all children to join: "KINDNESS TO ANIMALS CLUB A BRAND NEW CLUB FOR ALL BOYS AND GIRLS, WILL YOU BE AN ACTIVE, LIVEWIRE MEMBER?"[32] The invitation continued by asking: "There are all kinds of clubs, but what could be more fun than to share in doing good and being kind to all animal life?[33] The instructions for joining the club were listed. A creed consisted of three promises to be pledged to by each applicant:

1. I will feed my pets and take care of them as I should.
2. I will be kind to all animal life.
3. I will try to get others to do the same.[34]

The KTA program gradually faded from notice after a full year of monthly attention. The last invitation to join was in the December, 1956, issue.[35] In the October, 1957, issue the last KTA letter was

---

30 *CF*, LI (January, 1952), 22.

31 *CF*, LI (January, 1952), 22

32 Ibid.

33 Ibid.

34 Ibid.

35 *CF*, LV (December, 1956), 54.

published from a member.[36] Thus ended the second major zoophilic program sponsored by a Church auxiliary.

The Mutual Improvement Association has never sponsored a specific program on animals. As it is intended for youth in the Church over the age of twelve, concentrating on cultural and recreational development more than doctrine, this is understandable. There have been isolated lessons given on zoophily. One lesson was entitled, "Hunting and Fishing," and contained a strong appeal to kindness. Providing food was the only acceptable motive in killing animals, and this was to be subjected to rigorous precautions of safety and mercy before shooting. When varmints were killed, the admonition was to avoid developing an enjoyment of killing. Another lesson on "The Boy and the Gun" contended that neither the first nor second thought should be to kill after seeing a deer. The hunter must first consider the safety of shooting and the justice and mercy involved of shooting the animal.[37]

There have been infrequent articles on zoophily in the *Improvement Era*, which was the official publication of the Young Men's and Young Women's Mutual Improvement Associations of the Church until 1971. Two articles in 1920 and four in 1921 was the most concentrated coverage during the *Era's* history. The sentiment expressed in a short paragraph dealing with animals was that the time would come when "the nation's thinkers" would see that the only way "under heaven" to teach men to be merciful would be to do "kind acts a hundred times a day to the dumb creatures" that surround them.[38] Quoting from the "Humane Education Press Bureau," the *Era* admonished teachers to "have the right spirit in humane work" and thus "lay the foundation for thoughtfulness,

---

36 *CF*, LVI (October, 1957), 53.

37 Glenn L. Pearson, "Hunting and Fishing," and "The Boy and the Gun," *Handbook for Young Marrieds, 1962-63.* (Salt Lake City: The General Boards of the MIA, The Church of Jesus Christ of Latter-day Saints, 1962), 155-74.

38 *Improvement Era*, XXIII (February, 1920), 331. Hereafter *IE*.

unselfishness, in a word, humanitarianism."[39]

The principle that children who exercise kindness to the animal world would also show kindness to their fellow humans was a common concept mentioned in the *Era*.[40] It was said that "the humane man will not needlessly inflict pain upon the meanest thing that lives."[41] As a result of humane training children would become "better men and women," being "more humane, law-abiding, and in every respect more valuable citizens."[42]

Orson F. Whitney, a member of the Council of the Twelve of The Church of Jesus Christ of Latter-day Saints, referred to animals having souls. He stated that they were "to be eternally perpetuated." And Joseph Smith so believed, or he would not have said (as he is reputed to have said) concerning his favorite horse, when it died, that he expected to have it in eternity. Nor would he have uttered his heaven-inspired pronouncement that "the four beasts" seen in vision by John the Revelator (Rev. 4:6) "in describing heaven," "represent the glory of the classes of beings"—men, beasts, fowls, and creeping things—"in their destined order or sphere of creation, in the enjoyment of their eternal felicity" (Doctrine and Covenants 77:1-2).[43]

As mentioned previously, Joseph Fielding Smith referred to the eternal nature of animals in answering a theological question in the *Era*.[44] He also discussed the sin of killing "animals wantonly."[45]

---

39 *IE*, XXIII (August, 1920), 908.

40 *IE*, XXIV (April, 1921), 493, 532.

41 *IE*, XXIV (May, 1921), 649.

42 *IE*, XXIV (July, 1921), 783.

43 *IE*, XXX (August, 1927), 855.

44 *IE*, LXI (January, 1958), 16-17.

45 *IE*, LXIV (August, 1961), 568-69.

Two of the *Era's* predecessors, the *Young Women's Journal* and the *Contributor*, had little to say concerning zoophily. In fact, the *Young Women's Journal* had no mention of the subject, though it did print an article on "Pork Eating" one time. The article on pork quoted Brigham Young as having "denounced the eating of pork."[46] The *Contributor* had only three references to kindness to animals but did not specifically advocate zoophily. A lengthy article on "vegetarianism" did refer to the "slaughter" and bloodshed of animals as "unnatural" and "repulsive."[47] Hunting was condemned as being "productive of a callous indifference to the shedding of blood."[48] The balance of the article referred to the health benefits of the vegetarian diet.

A perusal of the *Relief Society Magazine*, a publication devoted to the women of the Church until 1970, revealed no articles of a zoophilic nature.

Lesson manuals for the men of the church have likewise yielded few lessons on zoophily. After quoting Joseph Smith's instructions concerning snakes on the Zion's Camp march, a lesson for the Melchizedek Priesthood in 1929 referred to Doctrine and Covenants 49:21 and gave a lengthy quote from "Taoist Teachings" on animals. The lesson concluded with the Taoist remark that, "in mind and understanding," there was no "wide gulf between any of the living species endowed with blood and breath, and, therefore, knowing this was so...the Taoist taught the animals wisdom."[49] Joseph Fielding Smith's commentary on the Doctrine and Covenants was used for priesthood

---

46 *Young Women's Journal*, II (April, 1900), 176-77.

47 *The Contributor*, IX (September, 1888), 423.

48 Ibid., 424.

49 *In the Realm of Quorum Activity Suggestions for Quorums of the Melchizedek Priesthood* (Independence, Mo.: Zion's Printing and Publishing Co., 1929), 78-79.

lessons in the 1940s and contained his comments on zoophily.[50] Also Joseph Fielding Smith's compilation of the teachings of his father, Joseph F. Smith, was used as a priesthood course of study in 1970-1972 and contained President Joseph F. Smith's comments on kindness to animals.[51]

The professional education arm of the Church, the seminaries and institutes of religion, has not had any specific lessons on this topic in their course outlines. One lesson without a title had an objective of thinking about the things around the students. A story entitled "A Boy, a Bird, and a Dog" related incidents of kindness to animal life.[52] Two consecutive lessons were on "Kindness," emphasizing kindness to animals.[53] Though the title of another lesson was "Florence Nightingale," the lesson was primarily on zoophily.[54]

The Church of Jesus Christ of Latter-day Saints has far more zoophilic teachings in an official capacity than other denominations in the United States. In addition to the premise that cruelty to animals breeds cruelty to humans, the Latter-day Saints have as added doctrine the principle that animals are to be resurrected and placed in kingdoms of heavenly glory with humans. As indicated by some authorities, this

---

50 Supra, CH & MR, I:210.

51 Supra, *Gospel Doctrine*, 266.

52 William A. Morton, *Lesson Book for the Religion Classes in The Church of Jesus Christ of Latter-day Saints, Second Grade* (n.p.: Deseret Book Co., 1925), 73-75.

53 Thomas L. Martin, *Lesson Book for the Religion Classes in The Church of Jesus Christ of Latter-day Saints, Fifth Grade, 1924-1925* ([Salt Lake City]: Deseret Book Co., 1924), 35-44.

54 Melvin C. and Amy Lyman Merrill, *Lesson Book for the Religion Classes in The Church of Jesus Christ of Latter-day Saints, Sixth Grade, 1925-1926* ([Salt Lake City]: Deseret Book Co.,1925), 63-66.

means that man may be accountable to God for the abusive treatment given to them on earth. Additionally, the Church's health code, known as the Word of Wisdom, admonished the use of meat "sparingly" to be used in times of winter, or cold weather, or famine. This is all tempered by the doctrine that man is divine, and animals are definitely of a lower sphere of existence and may be killed to supply food for man. These doctrines form the basis for the Latter-day Saint emphasis found lacking in other denominations.

Conclusion

The Church of Jesus Christ of Latter-day Saints has been in the forefront of a spiritual concern for the environment and especially the treatment of animals and birds. There have been sporadic bursts of official concern and prophetic counsel for members to treat all living creatures with kindness. This has been in stark contrast to much of the traditional Christian world, where animals are not considered to have spirits nor will they be resurrected. There have been individual religious people who have held otherwise, but in every church they are in the minority and have strong theological opposition from their leadership. Of course in the Latter-day Saint community there is not strong support for the official position. There is still a lot of ignorance on what the position of the scriptures and the prophets is on the subject of animals. I am encouraged by *Church News* editorials, comments, and letters from individual members. Stories by Douglas Thayer of BYU are inspiring and help to raise the consciousness of his readers. Other writers have touched on the subject in a positive way as well. Personally I have tried to be low-keyed because of my responsibilities as an Institute director for the Church. We are a practical church, and the Lord does not encourage radical behavior or teaching. I have been careful not to be judgmental of hunters and farmers who do not see things the way I do. But the fine line of behavior and teaching is to be set by our priesthood leaders, which I have followed and intend to continue doing so. Both their teachings and example of behavior should be considered wisely.

Since my original research on the topic many years ago, my perception has not changed much. I still feel that the prophets and scriptures teach that people should treat animals kindly. However, people are more important than animals and it seems clear that men can use animals for assistance in travel, food, protection, and companionship. When necessary animals may be killed to protect people from their attacks. They may also be killed for food, but the scriptures implore us not to unless necessary to sustain our lives.

Animals do have spirits and will be resurrected. We will be accountable for our treatment of animals and indeed may be able to communicate better with them about that judgment in the next life. Inordinate time, money, or energy should not be spent on animals to the detriment of our fellow humans. On the other hand, our attitude of gratitude towards animals will usually affect the way we treat all living creatures, including other people. There seems to be strong evidence that cruelty to animals can prepare for cruelty or unkindness to people. It is our responsibility to help bring peace to the earth and all of its living inhabitants. Our loving actions will affect animals and people alike to return and reflect that love to all. Our Father in Heaven indicates He would be very pleased with such actions and attitudes.

Individual decisions on euthanasia for animals, neutering, or otherwise physically changing an animal should be thoughtfully done. Prayer, conscience, the Spirit, and advice from others should all be factors in making such decisions. Vegetarianism is not to be preached in the Church according to the scriptures, but the practice is a personal matter and is left to the individual to decide within the bounds the Lord has set, including section 89 of the Doctrine and Covenants. We should do what we feel is best and what is not considered improper by priesthood leaders.

It is my prayer that this reminder of the Lord's teachings contained in this book will be of some help to people in bringing peace and understanding to all on the earth.

Appendix A

Kindness to Animals

"A righteous man regardeth the life of his beast; but the tender mercies of the wicked are cruel." So wrote the man of wisdom nearly three thousand years ago. Since that time how many unrighteous men have caused untold suffering among the poor, dumb animals! The dominion the Lord gave man over the brute creation has been, to a very large extent, used selfishly, thoughtlessly, cruelly. This is true even in the use and treatment of faithful beasts of burden, willing to serve their master as long as life remained. Besides the brutality thus manifested toward domestic animals there has been manifest in the human family the torturing instinct, to satiate which innocent, helpless creatures by untold millions, have been wantonly put to death. Even in this so-called enlightened age, this murderous spirit is still rampant. Only last summer, I am told, a member of a party visiting in the country came from the field one evening boasting that he had killed a porcupine with a club. One of the party, who believed that it is sinful needlessly to take the life of any creature, asked if he was sure the animal was dead. "Oh yes," was the reply, "I finished him." The questioner, however, had his doubts. The thought that the poor creature might still be suffering, and might continue to suffer for several days, so worked on his humane nature that he determined to ascertain for himself the true condition of the porcupine. Having inquired as to where the poor beast was, he made some excuse or other for riding out from camp, and went directly to the place. His conjectures were right. The animal had not been killed, but in a most brutal manner had been beaten into insensibility. His head was a mass of blood and bruises, and both eyes were gouged from their sockets. Though the poor animal was breathing with great effort, still there was a possibility of its lingering in this pitiful condition for a long time. However, as there could be no hope for it to recover, and even it if did, it would be totally blind, the young man concluded that it would be an act of mercy to end the animal's sufferings in instant death. Upon his return to the camp he told what he had done, and expressed in a kind but emphatic way his abhorrence at killing an innocent, harmless animal. The young man who had yielded to the torturing instinct took the lesson to heart, and vowed then and there that never again would he be guilty of such a barbarous act. Kindness to the whole animal creation and especially to all domestic animals, is not only a virtue that should be developed, but is the absolute duty of mankind. Children should be taught that Nature in all her forms is our Heavenly Father's great book of life. Furthermore, he who treats in a brutal manner a poor, dumb animal at that moment disqualifies himself for the companionship of the Holy Spirit; for the Lord will not sanction an unrighteous act, and it is an unrighteous thing to treat any creature cruelly. If the treatment be given in anger the result is the same, for anger itself is displeasing to the Lord, and the ill-treatment of the animal under such conditions, gives him double displeasure.

The Prophet Joseph Smith gives a beautiful lesson on kindness to animals as follows: We quote from his diary of May 26, 1834: "We crossed the Embarras river and encamped on a small branch of the same about one mile west. In pitching my tent we found three massasaugas or prairie rattlesnakes, which the brethren were about to kill, but I said, 'Let them alone—don't hurt them! How will the serpent ever lose its venom, while the servants of God possess the same disposition, and continue to make war upon it? Men must become harmless, before the brute creation; and when men lose their vicious dispositions and cease to destroy the animal race, the lion and the lamb can dwell together, and the suckling child can play with the serpent in safety!' The brethren took the serpents carefully on sticks and carried them across the creek. I exhorted the brethren not to kill a serpent, bird, or an animal of any kind during our journey unless it became necessary to preserve ourselves from hunger."

Such is the humane teaching of the Latter-day Prophet, and such should be the instruction given throughout the Church. This is the month in which a Sunday is set apart for the special purpose of teaching the necessity of kindness to animals. This instruction should not be confined to the children, but given to men and women as well; for-

"He prayeth well, who loveth well
Both man and bird and beast,
He liveth best who lovest best
All things both great and small;
For the dear God who loveth us,
He made and loveth all."

In the Yellowstone Park, where the use of guns and other deadly weapons is prohibited by law, and the law is carefully guarded by faithful soldiers whose duty is to enforce it, the animals and birds are becoming as tame and fearless of human beings, their deadliest foes, as domestic animals and barnyard fowls. The pretty mother deer, with her little ones, have almost lost their fear of man. The birds do not fly away with fright at the approach of men; even the brown, cinnamon and grizzly bears are friendly, some of them so tame as to take their food from the hands of men—all because, for a few years, they have not been hunted, shot at and slaughtered by the lords of creation. Thus it may be seen, in harmony with the sentiments expressed by the Prophet Joseph Smith, that if man did right, were humane and merciful toward animals, they would, in time, lose their fear and dread of him, and would also lose many, if not all, of their own bad traits. Animals are not cruel and vicious just for the fun of it, as is too often the case with man, but generally they are prone to destroy life only to appease their own hunger. It will be a blessed day when mankind shall accept and abide by the Christlike sentiment expressed by one of the poets in the following words: "Take not away the life you cannot give, For all things have an equal right to live."

Joseph F. Smith.[1]

---

1. Joseph F. Smith, "Kindness to Animals," *Juvenile Instructor* (February, 1912), 78-79.

Appendixes 2-4

2. *Ensign*, (Aug. 1972), 62-65.
3. *Ensign*, (Mar. 1977), 61-62.
4. *Church News* editorial, "Dominion over the Earth," Feb. 17, 1996, 16.

Bibliography

Books

Abel, Alan. *The Great American Hoax*. New York: Trident Press, 1966.

A Brief Exposition of the Established Principles and Relations of the United Society of Believers, Called Shakers. Hartford: Elihu Geer, 1850.

Ames, Evelyn. *A Glimpse of Eden*. Boston: Houghton Mifflin Co.: 1967.

Amory, Cleveland. *Man Kind? Our Incredible War on Wildlife*. New York: Harper & Row, 1974.

Andrews, Edward. *The People Called Shakers*. New York: Oxford University Press, 1953.

Aquinas, Thomas. *Summa Theologica.* 2 vols. Chicago: Encyclopedia Britannica, 1952.

Aquis, Ambrose. *God's Animals*. n.p.: Catholic Study for Animal Welfare, 1970.

Assisi, Francis. *The Little Flowers*. New York: E. P. Dutton and Company, 1951.

Austin, Philip. *Our Duty to Animals*. London: n.n., 1885.

Baldwin, Carey. *My Life with Animals*. Menlo Park, Ca.: Lane Book Co., 1964.

Baltzer, Eduard. *Vegetarianismus in der Bibel*. Norhausen: Forstemann, 1872.

Barber, Ian G., ed. *Earth Might Be Fair*. Englewood Cliffs: Prentice-Hall Inc., 1972.

Barkas, Janet. *The Vegetable Passion*. New York: Charles Scribner's Sons,1975.

Bartlett, Elisha. *Obedience to the Laws of Health, a Moral Duty*. Boston: J. A. Noble, 1838.

Bates, Joseph. *The Autobiography of Elder Joseph Sates*. Battle Creek Mich.: Seventh-Day Adventist Publishing Association, 1868.

Baumgardt, David. *Bentham: And the Ethics of Today*. Princeton: Princeton University Press, 1952.

Bayle, Pierre. *Historical and Critical Dictionary*. Indianapolis: Bobbs & Merrill, 1965.

Bell, Earnest. *An Afterlife for Animals*. London: Bell, n.d.

________*The Inner Life of Animals*. London: Bell, n.d.

________*Why Do Animals Exist?* London: Bell, n.d.

Bell, Martin. *The Way of the Wolf.* New York: The Seabury Press, 1970.

Bentham, Jeremy. *The Works of Jeremy Bentham*, 10 vols. New York: Russell & Russell, 1962.

Berman, Louis A. *Vegetarianism & the Jewish Tradition*. New York: KTAV Publishing House Inc., 1982.

Berrow, Capel.*A Lapse of Souls in a State of Preexistence*. London: n.n.,1762.

Bird, Herbert S. *Theology of Seventh-Day Adventism*. Grand Rapids: Wm. B. Eerdman's Publishing Co., 1961.

Bleibtreau, John N. *The Parable of the Beast*. New York: Macmillan, 1968.

Boas, George. *The Happy Beast*. Baltimore: Johns Hopkins Press, 1933.

Boone, Allen. *Letters to Strongheart.* Harrington Park, N.J.: Robert H. Summer, Publisher,1977.

Boone, J. Allen. *Kinship with All Life.* New York: Harper & Row, 1954.

Bourjaily, Vance. *The Unnatural Enemy.* New York: The Dial Press, 1963.

Bourne, F. W. *The Bible Christians: Their Origin and History*. London: Bible Christian Reading Room, 1905.

Briggs, Anna C. *For the Love of Animals.* Potomac Publishing Co.: n.p., 1990.

Brooks, Juanita, ed. *On the Mormon Frontier: The Diary of Hosea Stout, 1844-1861.* 2 vols. Salt Lake City: University of Utah Press, 1964.

________ and Robert G. Cleland, eds. *A Mormon Chronicle: The Diary of John D. Lee, 1848-1876.* 2 vols. San Marino: Huntington Library, 1955.

Browne, Peter. *Procedure, Extent, and Limits of Human Understanding.* London : n.n.,.1729.

Buckner, E. D. *Immortality of Animals and the Relation of Man as Guardian*. Philadelphia: George W. Jacobs & Co., 1903.

Butler, Joseph. *The Analogy of Religion*. Philadelphia: J. P. Lippincott, 1882.

Carr, Agnes. *The Animals and Birds Redeemed from Death: Their Eternal Glory.* San Francisco: n.n., 1953.

Carson, Gerald. *Cornflake Crusade.* New York: Rinehart and Co., 1957.

_______. *Men, Beasts, and Gods: A History of Cruelty and Kindness to Animals.* New York: Charles Scribner's Sons, 1972.

Clark, James R., ed. *Messages of the First Presidency.* 5 vols. Salt Lake City: Bookcraft, 1965-1970.

Clark, Stephen R. L. *The Moral Status of Animals.* New York: Oxford University Press, 1977.

Christman, Henry M. *Mahout.* Wheaton, Ill.: The Theosophical Publishing House, 1982.

Clarke, Frances E., ed. *Poetry's Plea for Animals.* Boston: Lothrop, Lee and Shepard Co., 1927.

Cobbe, Frances Power. *The Modern Rack.* London: S. Sonnenshchein, 1889.

Cocchi, Antoni. *The Pythagorean Diet.* London: R. Dodsley, 1745.

Cohen, Noah J. *Tsa'ar Ba'ale Hayim—The Prevention of Cruelty to Animals: Its Bases, Development and Legislation in Hebrew Literature.* Washington, D.C.: The Catholic University of America Press, 1959.

Coleman, Sydney H. *Humane Society Leaders in America.* Albany: The American Humane Association, 1924.

Collected from Living Witnesses in Union with the Church. Testimonies of the Life, Character, Revelations and Doctrines of Mother Ann Lee. Albany: Weed, Parson & Co., 1888.

Conference Reports. Salt Lake City: Deseret Book Company, 1897-1997.

Cooper, Sir William Earnshaw. *The Bloodguiltiness of Christendom.* London: Order of the Golden Age, n.d.

Cornaro, Luigi. *The Art of Living Long.* Milwaukee: W. F. Butler, 1905.

Coville, Marion E. *An Appeal Against Slaughter.* Syracuse: C. W. Bardeen, 1914.

Dahl, Paul, ed. *Journal of William Clayton.* Provo, Utah: J. Grant Stevenson, 1964.

Divine Book of Holy and Eternal Wisdom. Canterbury, N.H.: United Society, Called Shakers, and with the approbation of the leading Authority thereof, 1849.

Doctrine and Covenants. Salt Lake City: The Church of Jesus Christ of Latter-day Saints, 1952.

Dombrowski, Daniel A. *Hartshorne and the Metaphysics of Animal Rights.* State University of New York Press: Albany, 1988.

Doyley, Elizabeth. *An Anthology for Animal Lovers.* London: Collins, n.d.

Dunlavy, Joseph. *The Manifesto.* New York: Edward O. Jenkins, 1847.

Eads, H. L. *Shaker Sermons.* South Union, Ky.: n.n.,1889.

Eddy, Mary Baker. *Miscellaneous Writings, 1883-1896.* Boston: Trustees Under the Will of Mary Baker G. Eddy, [C. 1924]. Boston: 1875.

________ *Science and Health with Key to the Scriptures.* Trustees Under the Will of Mary Baker G. Eddy, 1875.

________ *Unity of Good.* Boston: Trustees Under the Will of Mary Baker G. Eddy, [1919].

Editorial Committee. *Medical Papers.* Mountain View, Calif.: Pacific Press Publishing Association, 1931.

Essene Gospel of Jesus, The. Santa Monica, Ca.: The Edenite Society, 1978.

Evans, Edward Payson. *The Criminal Persecution and Capital Punishment of Animals.* New York: E. P. Dutton, 1906.

________ *Evolutionary Ethics and Animal Psychology*. London: Heinemann, 1897.

Evans, Frederick Wm. *Shakers: Compendium of the Origin, History, Principles, Rules and Regulations, Government and Doctrines of the United Society of Believers in Christ's Second Appearing.* New Lebanon, N.Y.: 1867.

Facklam, Margery. *Wild Animals, Gentle Women.* New York: Harcourt Brace Jovanovich, 1978.

Fairholme, Edward G. and Wellesley Pain. *A Century of Work for Animals: A History of the R.S.P.C.A., 1824-1924.* London: John Murray, 1924.

Farbridge, Maurice H. *Studies in Biblical and Semitic Symbolism.* London: Kegan, Paul, Trench, Trubner, and Co., 1923.

Ferm, Vergilius. *Encyclopedia of Morals* .New York: Philosophical Library, 1956.

__________ *Encyclopedia of Religion.* New York: Philosophical Library, 1945.

Ferrier, J. Todd. *On Behalf of the Creatures.* London: Order of the Cross, 1947.

Fletcher, Colin. *The Winds of Mara.* New York: Alfred A. Knopf, 1973.

Fletcher, Ralph. *A Few Notes on Cruelty to Animals.* London: n.n., 1846.

Foster, T. *Philozoia.* Brussells: n.n., 1839.

Fox, Michael W. *Animals Have Rights, Too.* New York: Continuum, 1991.

__________ *Returning to Eden.* New York: The Viking Press, 1980.

Franklin, Benjamin. *The Autobiography of Benjamin Franklin.* n.p.: P.F. Collier and Son, 1909.

Fremantle, Anne. *The Age of Belief.* New York: The New American Library, 1959.

Funk and Wagnalls. *New Standard Dictionary.* New York: Funk and Wagnalls, 1960.

Geist, Valerius. *Mountain Sheep and Man in the Northern Wilds.* Ithaca: Cornell University Press, 1975.

General Boards of the MIA. *Handbook for Young Marrieds, 1962-63.* Salt Lake City: The Church of Jesus Christ of Latter-day Saints, 1962.

General Church Board of Education. *Lesson Book for the Religion Classes in The Church of Jesus Christ of Latter-day Saints.* 16 vols. Salt Lake City: Deseret Book Co., 1924-26.

Godlovitch, Stanley and John and Rosalind Harris, eds. *Animals, Men and Morals.* New York: Grove Press, 1972.

Gompertz, Lewis. *Moral Inquiries on the Situation of Man and Brutes.* London: n.n., 1824.

Graham, Sylvester. *Science of Human Life*. Boston: Capen, Lyon and Webb, 1858.

________*The Aesculapian Tablets of the Nineteenth Century*. Providence: Weedon & Gory, 1834.

Grzimek, Bernhard and Michael. *Serengeti Shall Not Die.* New York: Ballantine Books, Inc. 1973.

Hallet, Jean-Pierre. *Animal Kitabu*. New York: Random House, 1967.

Hallie, Philip P. *The Paradox of Cruelty.* Middletown, Conn.: Wesleyan University Press, 1969.

Harwood, Dix. *Love for Animals and How It Developed in Great Britain*. New York: n.n, 1828.

Haskett, William J. *Shakerism Unmasked or the History of the Shakers*. Pittsfield: Published by the Author, 1828.

Hastings, James, ed. *Encyclopedia of Religion and Ethics.* 12 vols. New York: Charles Scribners & Sons, 1951.

Hawkins, T. S. *The Soul of an Animal.* London: Allen & Unwin, 1921.

Hearne, Vicki. *Animal Happiness.* New York: Harper Collins, 1994.

Heath, Harvard S., ed. *In the World: The Diaries of Reed Smoot.* Salt Lake City: Signature Books, 1997.

Helps, Sir Arthur. *Some Talk about Animals and Their Masters*. London: n.n., 1873.

Herriot, James. *All Creatures Great and Small.* New York: St. Martin's Press, 1972

Herriot James. *All Things Wise and Wonderful.* New York: St. Martin's Press, 1977.

Hildrop, John. *Free Thoughts upon the Brute Creation.* London: n.n., 1742.

Holy Scriptures. Independence, Mo.: Herald Publishing Co., 1948.

Hume, C. W. *The Status of Animals in the Christian Religion*. London: Universities Federation for Animal Welfare, 1957.

Huson, Hobart, ed. *Pythagoron: The Religious, Moral, and Ethical Teachings of Pythagoras.* n.p. n.n., 1947.

Hymns. Salt Lake City: The Church of Jesus Christ of Latter-day Saints, 1966.

In the Realm of Quorum Activity. Suggestions for Quorums of the Melchizedek Priesthood. Independence, Mo. : Zion's Printing and Publishing Co., 1929.

Jones, Gerald E. and Scott S. Smith. *Animals and the Gospel.* Thousand Oaks, Ca.: Millennial Publications, 1980.

Joy, Charles R. *The Animal World of Albert Schweitzer.* Boston: The Beacon Press, 1950.

Kalechofsky, Roberta. *Haggadah for the Liberated Lamb*. Marblehead, Mass.: Micah Publications, 1985.

Kimball, Edward L., ed. *The Teachings of Spencer W. Kimball.* Salt Lake City: Bookcraft, 1982.

Kimball, Stanley B. *Heber C. Kimball: Mormon Patriarch and Pioneer.* Urbana: University of Illinois Press, 1981.

Kindness to Animals. Philadelphia: The American Sunday School Union, 1845.

Kingsford, Anna and Edward Maitland. *Essays and Addresses in Vegetarianism.* London: Watkins, 1912.

Knowles, Dom David. *The Religious Orders in England.* 3 vols. Cambridge: Cambridge University Press, 1959.

Krause, Flora Helm. *Manual of Moral and Humane Education.* Chicago: R. R. Donnelly and Sons, Co., 1910.

Lambe, William. *Reports of the Effects of a Peculiar Regimen.* London: J. Mawman, 1809.

Larson, A. Karl and Katherine Miles Larson. *Diary of Charles Lowell Walker.* 2 vols. Logan, Ut.: Utah State University Press, 1980.

Lathrop, Dorothy. *Let Them Live.* New York: Macmillan and Co., 1965.

Lawrence, John. *A Philosophical Treatise on Horses, and on the Moral Duties of Man towards the Brute Creation.* London: H. D. Symonds, 1802.

Lecky, William E. H. *History of European Morals.* 2 vols. New York: D. Appleton & Co., 1895.

Lefevre, Jules. *A Scientific Investigation into Vegetarianism.* London: London Vegetarian Society, n.d.

Lewinsohn, Richard. *Animals, Men and Myths.* New York: Harper and Brothers, 1954.

Linzey, Andrew. *Christianity and the Rights of Animals.* New York: Crossroad, 1987.

______*Animal Rights: A Christian Assessment of Man's Treatment of Animals.* London: SCM Press, 1976.

Lloyd, Bertram. *The Great Kinship: An Anthology of Humanitarian Poetry.* London: Alien & Unwin, 1921.

Lobb, Theophile. *A Treatise on Dissolvements of the Stone.* London: J. Buckland, 1730.

Long, Herbert Strainge. *A Study of the Doctrine of Metempsychosis in Greece from Pythagoras to Plato.* Princeton: Princeton University Press, 1948.

Luther, Martin. *Luther's Works.* 12 vols. St. Louis: Concordia Publishing House, 1960.

Lydecker, Beatrice. *What the Animals Tell Me.* San Francisco: Harper & Row, 1977.

Macawley, J. *A Plea for Mercy to Animals.* London: n.n., 1881.

Mace, Aurelia G. *The Alethis: Spirit of Truth*. Farmington, Maine: Knowlson, McLeary and Company, 1899.

Martinengo-Ceseresco, *Countess Evelyn: The Place of Animals in Human Thought*. New York: Scribners & Sons, 1909.

Marvin, Frederic Rowland. *Christ among the Cattle*. Troy, N.Y.: Patroets Book Co., 1908.

McCrea, Roswell Cheney. *The Humane Movement*. New York: Columbia University Press, 1910.

McGiffert, A. C. *Protestant Thought before Kant*. New York: Harper Brothers, 1962.

Merrill, Joseph F. *The Truth Seeker and Mormonism*. Independence, Mo.: Zion's Printing and Publishing Co., 1946.

Metcalfe, William. *Bible Testimony on Abstinence from the Flesh of Animals as Food*. Philadelphia: J. Metcalfe & Co., 1840.

Montaigne, Michel. *Essays: Great Books of the Western World*. Vol. 25. Chicago: Encyclopedia Britannica, 1952.

Moore, Thomas. *Utopia*. New York: P. F. Collier & Son, 1910.

Morrell, Jeanette McKay. *Highlights in the Life of President David O. McKay*. Deseret Book Co., 1966.

Morris, Richard and Michael W. Fox, eds. *On the Fifth Day: Animal Rights and Human Ethics*. Washington D.C.: Acropolis Press, 1978.

Morris, Robert. *A Reasonable Plea for the Animal Creation*. London: M. Cooper, 1746.

Moss, A. W. *Valiant Crusade*. London: Casell & Co., 1961.

Mowat, Farley. *The Dog Who Wouldn't Be*. Boston: Atlantic-Little, Brown, 1957.

Mulder, William and Russell Mortenson. *Among the Mormons*. New York: Alfred A. Knopf, 1958.

Neihardt, John G. *Black Elk Speaks*. Lincoln: University of Nebraska Press, 1961.

Newman, Richard. *Bless All They Creatures Lord: Prayers for Animals*. New York: Macmillan, 1982.

Nibley, Preston. *Presidents of the Church*. Salt Lake City: Deseret Book Co., 1959.

Nicholson, Edward Bryon. *The Rights of Animals, A New Essay in Ethics*. London: n.n., 1879.

Niven, Charles D. *History of the Humane Movement*. London: Johnson Publications, 1967.

Noss, John. *Man's Religions*. New York: Macmillan & Co., 1956.

O'Kelly, James. *An Essay on Negro Slavery*. Philadelphia: n.n., 1789.

Oswald, John. *The Cry of Nature*. n.p.: n.n., 1791.

Ovid. *Metempsychosis*. Cambridge: Harvard University Press, 1961.
Oxford English Dictionary. Vol. XII. Oxford: University Press, 1961.
Passmore, John. *Man's Responsibility for Nature*. London: Duckworth, 1974.
Paterson, D.A. and Richard Ryder, eds. *Animal Rights: A Symposium*. London: Centaur, 1979.
Parton, J. *The Life of Horace Greeley*. New York: Mason Bros., 1855.
Pearl of Great Price. Salt Lake City: The Church of Jesus Christ of Latter-day Saints, 1965.
Plotinus. *Enneads*. Boston: Charles T. Ranford, 1916.
Plutarch. *Lives and Writings*. Vol. X. New York: Colonial Co., 1905.
Porphyry. *Abstinence from Animal Food*. N.p.: Barnes & Noble, 1965.
Pratt, Parley P. *Voice of Warning*. Independence, Mo.: Zion's Printing and Publishing Co., 1928.
Primatt, Humphrey. *A Dissertation on the Duty of Mercy and Sin of Cruelty to Animals*. London: n.n., 1776.
Questions on Doctrine. Washington, D.C.: Review and Herald Publishing Association, 1957.
Radhakrishnan, Sarvepalli and Charles A. Moore. *A Source Book in Indian Philosophy*. Princeton: Princeton University Press, 1957.
________. *Indian Philosophy*. New York: Macmillan, 1929.
Regan, Tom. *The Case for Animal Rights*. Berkeley: University of California Press, 1983.
Regan, Tom, and Peter Singer, eds. *Animal Rights and Human Obligations*. Englewood Cliffs, Prentice Hall Inc., 1976.
Regenstein, Lewis G. *Replenish the Earth*. New York: Crossroad, 1991.
Rice, Berkeley. *The Other End of the Leash*. Boston: Little, Brown and Co., 1968.
Rich, Ben E. *Scrapbook of Mormon Literature*. 2 vols. N.p.: Ben E. Rich, n.d.
Rickaby, Joseph. *Political and Moral Essays*. New York: Benziger, 1902.
Riegell Robert E. *Young America: 1830-1840.* Norman: University of Oklahoma Press, 1940.
Ritson, Joseph. *An Essay on Abstinence from Animal Food as a Moral Duty*. London: R. Phillips, 1802.
Roberts, Alexander, and James Donaldson, eds. *Ante-Nicene Fathers*. 10 vols. New York & Grand Rapids: William B. Eerdman's, 1951.
Roberts, Catherine. *Science, Animals, and Evolution*. Westport, Ct.: Greenwood Press, 1980.
Robinson, Dores Eugene. *The Story of Our Health Message*. Nashville: Southern Publishing Association, 1943.
Romney, Thomas C. *The Life of Lorenzo Snow*. Salt Lake City: Deseret News Co., 1955.

Rosen, Steven. *Food for the Spirit*. New York: Bala Books, 1987.
Rosten, Leo, ed. *Religions in America*. New York: Simon & Schuster, 1963.
Rowan, Andrew N. *Of Mice, Models, & Men*. Albany: State University of New York Press, 1984.
Rowley, Francis H. *The Humane Idea*. Boston: American Humane Society, 1912.
Rudd, Geoffrey L. *Why Kill for Food*? Wilmslow, Cheshire: Vegetarian Society, 1956.
Ruesch, Hans. *Slaughter of the Innocent*. New York: Bantam Books, 1978.
Salt, Henry S. *Animal's Rights Considered in Relation to Social Progress*. New York: Harcourt and Brace & Co., 1922.
_________ *Cruelties of Civilization: A Programme of Humane Reform*. London: Reeves and Turner, 1897.
_________ *Humanities of Diet*. Manchester: Vegetarian Society, 1914.
_________ *The Creed of Kinship*. New York: E.P. Dutton & Co., 1935.
_________ *The Logic of Vegetarianism*. London: Bell, 1906.
Scoby, Donald R., ed. *Environmental Ethics*. Minneapolis: Burgess Publishing Co., 1971.
Sbordone, Francesco, ed. *Physiologus*. Rome: Albrighi, Segati et al., 1936.
Schaff, Philip. *History of the Christian Church*. 8 vols. Grand Rapids, Mich.: Wm. Eerdman's Publishing Co., 1950.
Scheffer, Victor B. *A Voice for Wildlife*. New York: Charles Scribner's Sons, 1974.
Schlesinger, Arthur M. *The American as Reformer*. Cambridge: Harvard University Press, 1950.
Schochet, Elijah Judah. *Animal Life in Jewish Tradition*. New York: KTAV Publishing House, Inc., 1984.
Schweitzer, Albert. *Civilization and Ethics*. 2 vols. London: Adam & Charles Black, 1949.
Schweitzer, Albert. *Reverence for Life*. Ed. Thomas Kiernan. New York: Philosophical Library, 1965.
Sears, Clara Endicott, comp. *Gleanings from Old Shaker Journals*. Boston: Houghton, Mifflin Co., 1916.
Seneca, Lucius. *The Epistles*. Cambridge: Harvard University Press, 1943.
Seraphim, Sister. *All God's Creatures*. New York: Dodd, Mead & Co., 1966.
Shaw, Thomas. *The Bible Christians*. London: Epworth Press, 1965.
Short, William J. *Saints in the World of Nature*. Rome: Pontificia Universitas Gregoriana, 1983.
Shultz, William J. *The Humane Movement in the United States, 1910-1922*. New York: Columbia University Press, 1924.

Simoons, F. J. *Eat Not This Flesh: Food Avoidances in the Old World.* Madison: University of Wisconsin Press, 1961.

Singer, Peter. *Animal Liberation*. New York: Avon Books, 1975.

________ *The Expanding Circle*. New York: Farrar, Straus & Giroux., 1981.

________,ed. *In Defense of Animals.* New York: Basil Blackwell Inc., 1985.

Smith, John. *Fruits and Farinaca the Proper Food of Man*. New York: Fowler and Wells, 1854.

Smith, Joseph. *History of The Church of Jesus Christ of Latter-day Saints*, Ed B. H. Roberts. 7 vols. 2nd ed revised. Salt Lake City: Deseret Book Company, 1959.

Smith, Joseph Fielding. *Answers to Gospel Questions*. 5 vols. Salt Lake City-Deseret BookCo., 1957-1966.

________ *Church History and Modern Revelation*. 4 vols. Salt Lake City: Council of the Twelve Apostles of The Church of Jesus Christ of Latter-day Saints, 1947-1950.

________ *Man: His Origin and Destiny*. Salt Lake City: Deseret Book Co., 1954.

________ *Signs of the Times*. Salt Lake City: Deseret Book Co., 1964.

Smith, Joseph Fielding Jr. & John J. Stewart. *The Life of Joseph Fielding Smith*. Salt Lake City: Deseret Book Co., 1972.

Stevens, Paul Drew. *Real Animal Heroes*. Chico, Ca.: Sharp & Dunnigan, 1988.

Stiller, Herbert and Margot. *Animal Experimentation and Animal Experimenters*. Nimes: AGM, 1977.

The Church and Kindness to Animals. London: Burns & Gates, n.d.

The Divine Book of Holy and Eternal Wisdom. Canterbury, N.H.: United Society, called Shakers, 1849.

Tonna, Charlotte E. B. P. *Kindness to Animals*. Philadelphia: American Sunday School Union, 1845.

Trine, Ralph Waldo. *Every Living Creature*. New York: T. Y. Crowell & Co., 1899.

Turner, E. S. *All Heaven in a Rage.* New York: St. Martin's Press, 1965.

Tyler, Alice Felt. *Freedom's Ferment*. Minneapolis: University of Minnesota Press,1944.

Walton, Harold M. *Medical Papers*. Mountain View, Calif.: Pacific Press Publishing Assoc.

Ward-Harris, Joan. *Creature Comforts*. New York: St. Martin's Press, 1979.

Watson, Elden, ed. *Manuscript History of Brigham Young, 1846-1847.* Salt Lake City: Elden J. Watson, 1971.

Watt, George D., et al. *Journal of Discourses*. 26 vols. London: Latter-day Saint Book Depot, 1854-1886.

Webster's Third New International Dictionary. Springfield: G. & C. Merriam Co., 1966.

Wesley, John. *Sermons on Several Occasions*. Vol. 2. New York: J. Soule & T. Mason, 1818.

_________ *The Works of John Wesley*. 14 vols. London: Wesleyan Conference Office, 1872.

Westbeau, Georges H. *Little Tyke*. Mountain View, Calif.: Pacific Press Publishing Association, 1956

White, Anna and Leila S. Taylor. *Shakerism: Its Meaning and Message*. Columbus, Ohio: Fred J. Heer, 1904.

White, Ellen G. *Counsels on Diet and Foods*. Washington, D. C.: Review and Herald Publishing Association, 1946.

________ *Ministry of Healing*. Washington, D.C.: Review and Herald Publishing Association, n.d.

________ *Patriarchs and Prophets*. Washington, D. C.: Review and Herald Publishing Association, 1958.

Widtsoe, John A. *Joseph Smith*. Salt Lake City: Deseret Book Co., 1951.

_________, and Leah D. Widtsoe. *The Word of Wisdom*. Salt Lake City: Deseret News Press, 1938.

Williams, Howard. *The Ethics of Diet*. London: F. Pitman and John Heywood, 1883.

Windeatt, Philip. *The Hunt and the Anti-Hunt*. London: Pluto Press Ltd., 1982.

Wood, John G. *Man and Beast, Here and Hereafter*. London: n.n., 1874.

Woolman, John. *The Journal of John Woolman*. New York: P. F. Collier & Son, 1909.

Yonge, C.D., trans. *Works of Philo Judeaus*, 4 vols. London: Henry G. Bohn, 1854.

Youatt, William. *The Obligation and Extent of Humanity to Brutes*. London: Longman, Orme, Brown, Green, and Longmans, 1839.

Young, John R. *Memoirs of John R. Young*. Salt Lake City: Deseret News, 1920.

Articles and Periodicals

Altshuler, S.S. "The Historical and Biological Evolution of Human Diet," *American Journal of Digestive Diseases*, I (1934), 215.

"A Moral Faculty in Animals," *The Contributor,* IV (May, 1892), 318.

Amory , C. "Speaking Out: Science is Needlessly Cruel to Animals," *Saturday Evening Post*, CCXXX (July 27, 1963), 10.

Anderson, Erica. "God Bless All Living Beings," *Ladies Home Journal*, LXXX (December, 1963), 26-28.

Animaldom [Philadelphia, Pa.], 1930-1940.

Animal Herald [New Orleans, La.], 1890-1892.

Animal Life [Columbus, Ohio], 1944-1950.

Animal Life [Toronto, Ontario], 1911-1920.

Animal Protector [Cleveland, Ohio], 1946-1950.

Animal Rescue League Report [Boston, Mass.], 1900-1931.

Animals Defender & Zoophilist [London, England], 1881.

Animal World and Advocate of Humanity [London], 1869-1919.

Brigham Young University Studies, Provo, Utah, 1969.

Buchmiller, Gordon A. "Wanton Killing of Animals Denounced," *Church News,* (Oct. 7, 1978), 14-15.

Christian Vegetarian [Los Angeles], 1948.

Church News LDS Serviceman's Edition [Salt Lake City, Utah], March 15, 1946.

Children's Friend [Salt Lake City, Utah], 1901-1970.

Cobbe, Frances Power. "Zoophily," *Cornhill*, XLVI (March, 1882), 279-88.

Dore, Clement. "An examination of Soul-Making Theodicy," *American Philosophical Quarterly*, VII (April, 1970), 128-30

"Emphatic Fallacy," *America*, CI (August, 1959), 567.

Evening and Morning Star [Independence Mo], 1832-33.

"Father Rickaby's Political and Moral Essays.," *Month* (August, 1903), 213-14.

Geogheagan, William Davidson. "Albert Schweitzer's Covenant with Life," *Religion in Life*, 256.

Hardine, Mervyn G. and Hulda Crooks. "Non Flesh Dietaries," *Journal of the American Dietetic Association*, XLIII (December, 1963), 545-58.

Hart, Edward L. "Processional," *BYU Studies* 34:1 (1994), 30-31.

Hickman, Russell. "Vegetarian and Octagon Company," *Kansas Historical Quarterly*, II (November, 1933), 377-85.

Hoff, Rebel E., and John F. Fulton. "The Centenary of the First American Physiological Society Founded at Boston by William A. Alcott and Sylvester Graham," *Bulletin* of the Institute of the History of Medicine, V, 1937.

Humane Advocate [Chicago, Illinois], 1905-1919.
Humane Alliance [Chicago, Illinois], 1873-1899.
Humane Appeal [Cincinatti, Ohio], 1879-1881.
Humane Educator [Honolulu, Hawaii], 1900-1901.
Humane Educator [Cincinatti, Ohio], 1887-1894.
"Humane Killing," *Business Week*, MDXXXIX (February 28, 1959), 30.
Humanitarian [New York, New York], 1915-1919.
Humanitarian League [New York City, New York, 1891-1897.
Humane Journal [St. Paul, Minn]l, 1923-1935.
Hume, C. W. "The Religious Attitude Towards Animals," *LI* (April, 1953), 262-68.
Improvement Era [Salt Lake City, Utah], 1897-1970.
Inquiry [Boston, Mass.], Vol. 22 (Summer 1979), issue on Animal Rights., 1-247.
Instructor [Salt Lake City, Utah], 1930-1970.
"Isms of Forty Years Ago," *Harper's New Monthly Magazine*, LX (January, 1880), 190-91.
Jones, Gerald E. "The Gospel and Animals" *Ensign* (Aug. 1972), 62-65.
______ "The Beginnings of Latter-day Saint Concern for Animals" *Reverence of Life,* I (June 1972), 5-10.
_______"Brigham Young and Associates Concerning Animals," *The Animal Stewardship,* I (May 1973)
_______"El Evangelio y los animales," *Liahona*, 19 (June 1973), 36-39, 44.
_______"Where Do Animals Fit in the Eternal Plan of Things," *Ensign*, 7 (Mar. 1977), 61-62.
_______"Reverence for Life in Religion: Eastern and Western Views," in *Deity and Death,* ed. by Spencer Palmer, Provo, BYU Religious Studies, 1978. 107-120.
_______"The Place of Animals in Christian America," *Between the Species: A Journal of Ethics*, Vol. 1 (Spring, 1985), 15-20.
_______"Zoophily in Mormonism,"*Restoration,* Vol. 4 (October 1985), 1, 7-10.
_______ "The Latter-day Saints, The Seventh-Day Adventist and the Christian Scientist Perspectives: Sacred Cow or Sacrificial Lamb": *Religious Perspectives on Animals*. San Francisco: SPCA 1986., 18-20.
_______"The Place of Animals in Three American Churches," *Between the Species: A Journal of Ethics,* Vol. 2 (Fall 1986), 174-183.
Journal of Zoophily [Philadelphia, Pa.], 1891-1904.
Juvenile Instructor [Salt Lake City, Utah], 1866-1929.
LeDuc, Thomas H. "Grahamites: a History," XX (1939), 189-91.
Mendel, Lafayette B, "Some Historical Aspects of Vegetarianism," *The Popular Science Monthly*, LXIV (March, 1904), 457-46.

Milgrom, Jacob. "The Biblical Diet Laws as an Ethical System," *Interpretation,* 17 (1963), 288-301.

Mormon Forum. "How to show love, respect for animals." *Church News*, (June 19, 1983), 15.

Murray, John. "Animals in Theology," *A Catholic Dictionary of Theology*. London: Thomas Nelson Sons, 1962.

Naylor, Mildred V. "Sylvester Graham," *Annals of Medical History,* Third Series IV (May, 1942), 3.

National Humane Educator [Cincinnatti, Ohio], 1893-1901.

National Humane Journal [Chicago, Illinois], 1872-1917.

National Humane Review [New York City, New York], 1875-1909.

Our Animals [San Francisco, Calif], 1907-1920.

Our Dumb Animals [Boston, Mass.], 1868-1940.

Our Fellow Creatures [Chicago, Illinois], 1894-1902.

Our Four-footed Friends and How We Treat Them [Boston, Mass], 1902-1910.

Packard, Sandra Bradford. "Animals," *Encyclopedia of Mormonism,* New York: McMillan Publishing Co., Vol 1., 42-43.

Paine Thomas. "Cruelty to Animals Exposed," *The Pennsylvania Magazine*, I (May, 1775),

"Progress of Zoophilism," *The Saturday Review* (August 28, 1886), 290-91.

Progress Today [London], 1909.

Ratcliffe, J. D. "Vivesection, An Explosive Issue Again," *Reader's Digest*, LXXVIII (March, 1961), 56-61.

Schleslinger, Arthur M. "A Dietary Interpretation of American History," *Proceedings of the Massachusetts Historical Society*, LXVIII (1944-1948), 200-202.

Schweitzer, Albert. "The Problem of Ethics for Twentieth Century Man," *Saturday Review*, XXXVI (June 13, 1953), 11.

Shryock, Richard H. "Sylvester Graham and the Popular Health Movement," *Mississippi Valley Historical Review*, XVIII (September, 1831), 172-83.

Steams, Bertha-Monica. "Reform Periodical and Female Reformers," *American Historical Review*, XXXVII (n.d.)

The Carpenter [Madison, Wisconsin], I (1969)

Thayer, Douglas. "The Rabbit Hunt," *BYU Studies,* 22 (Winter, 1969), 198-208.

______. "Opening Day," *Under the Cottonwoods*. Provo, Ut. Frankson Books, 1977.

Times and Seasons [Nauvoo, Illinois], 1839-1846.

Vegetarian [Chicago, Illinois], 1896-1941.

Vegetarian [New York City, New York], 1895-1899.

Vegetarian Advocate [London], 1848-1852.

Vegetarian Messenger [London], 1849-1850.

Vegetarian News [London], 1921-1958.

"Viewpoint: Dominion Over the Earth," *Church News*, (Feb. 17, 1996), 16.
Young, Lorenzo Dow. "Biography of Lorenzo Dow Young," *Utah Historical Quarterly*, XIV (1946)

Unpublished Manuscripts

Chase, Daryl. "The Early Shakers: An Experiment in Religious Communism." Unpublished dissertation, University of Chicago, 1936.
"Journal History of The Church of Jesus Christ of Latter-day Saints," 1831-1971 in the Church Historian's Library, Salt Lake City, Utah.
Packard, Sandra Bradford. "The Salvation of Animals," 125 pp. Mss. ©. 1988).
Packer, Boyd K. "The Ideal Teacher." Distributed by Seminaries and Institutes of Religion, Provo, Utah, June 28, 1962. (Mimeographed.)
McAllister, James D. T. "Autobiography and Diary of J. D. T. McAllister." Brigham Young University Library, Provo, Utah. (Typed manuscript.)
Walker, William B. "The Health Reform Movement in the United States." Unpublished dissertation, Johns Hopkins University, 1955.

Index